DOUBLE
by
Marilyn R. Rosenberg
DOUBLE
by
Marilyn R. Rosenberg
I0836762

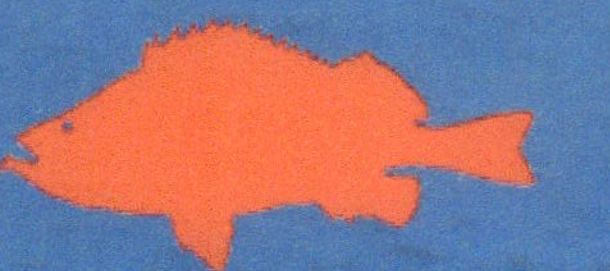

ISBN 9781938521782

LUNA BISONTE PRODS
137 Leland Ave
Columbus OH 43214 USA

www.lulu.com/spotlight/lunabisonteprods

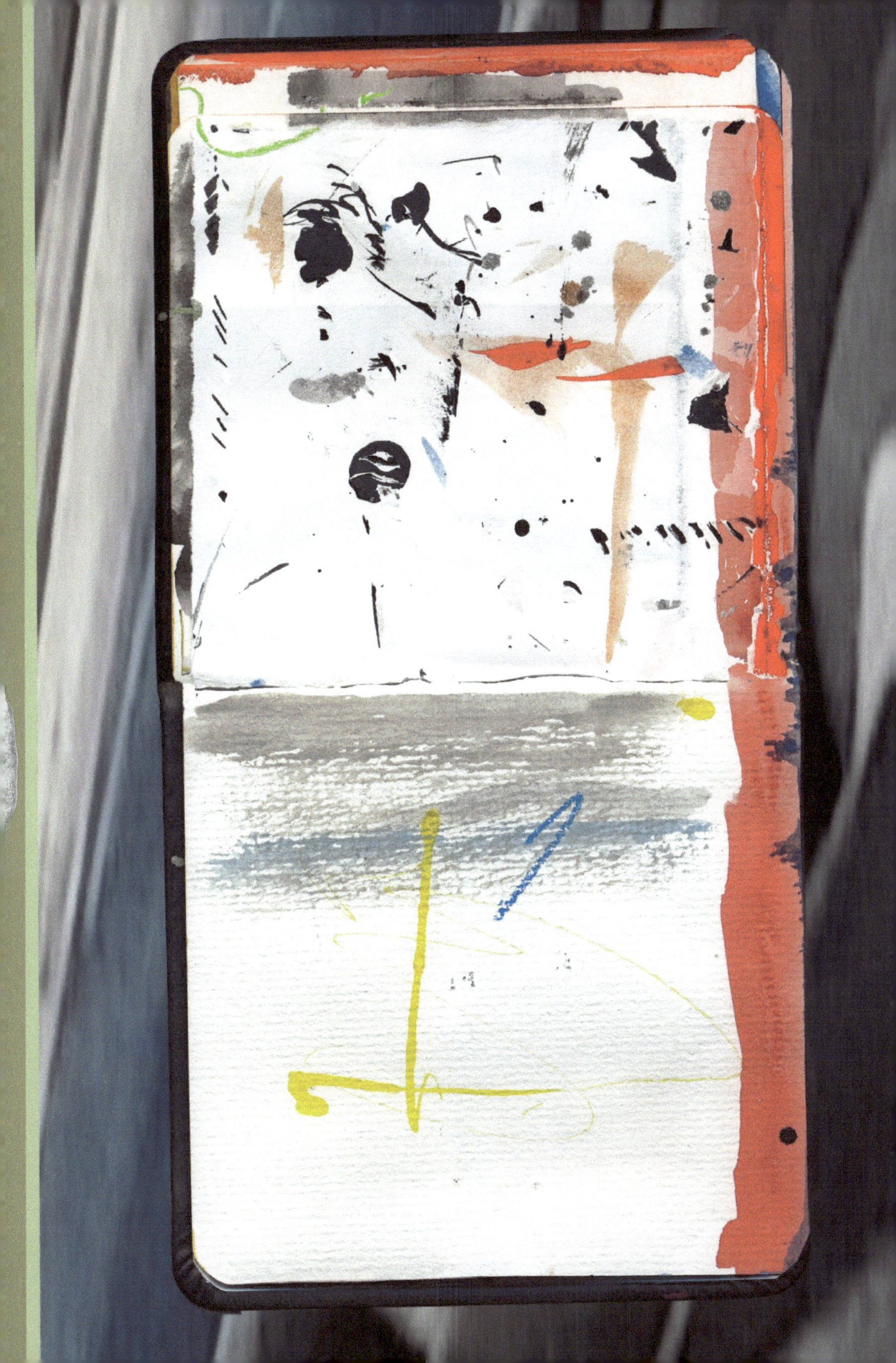

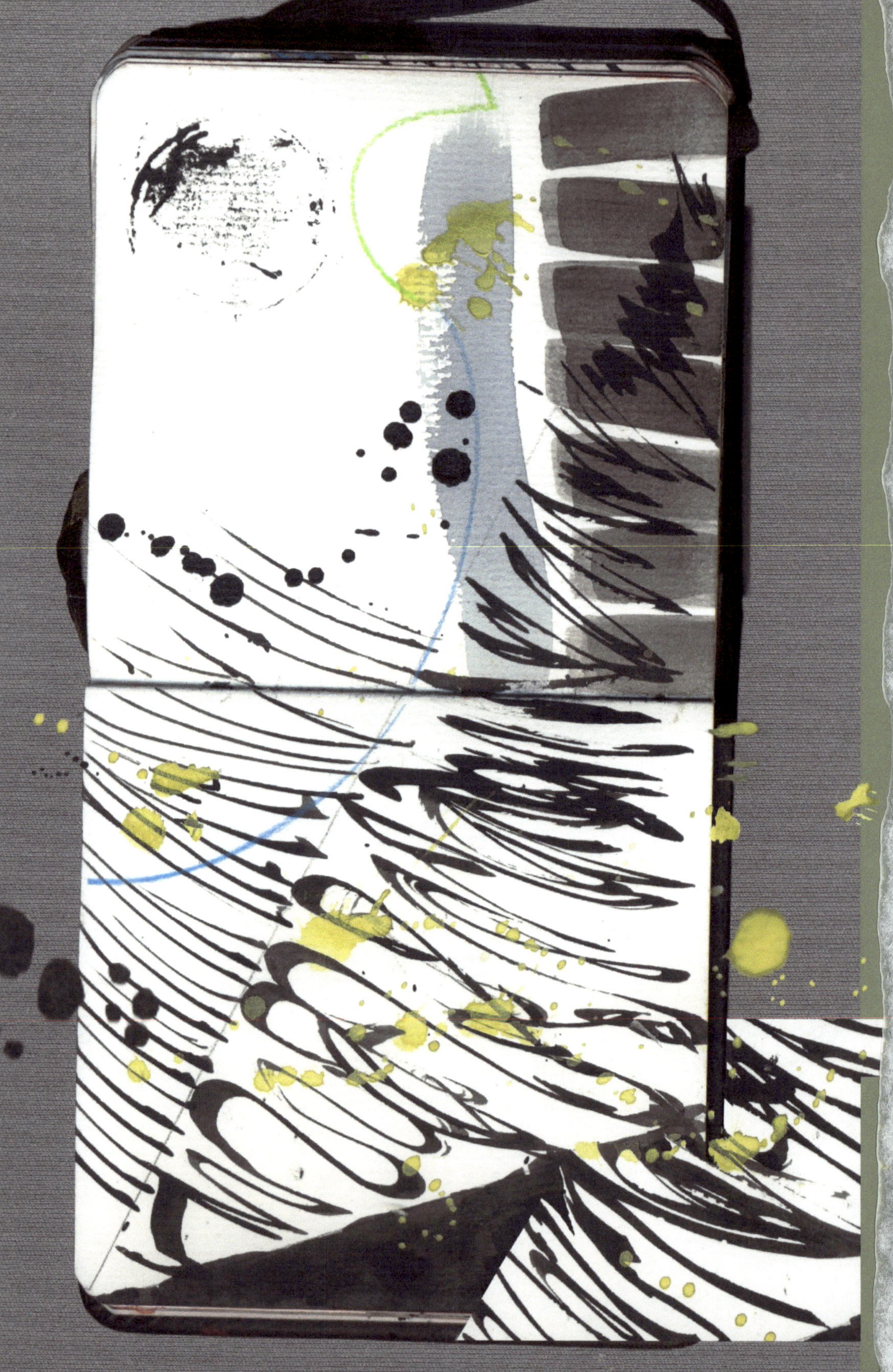

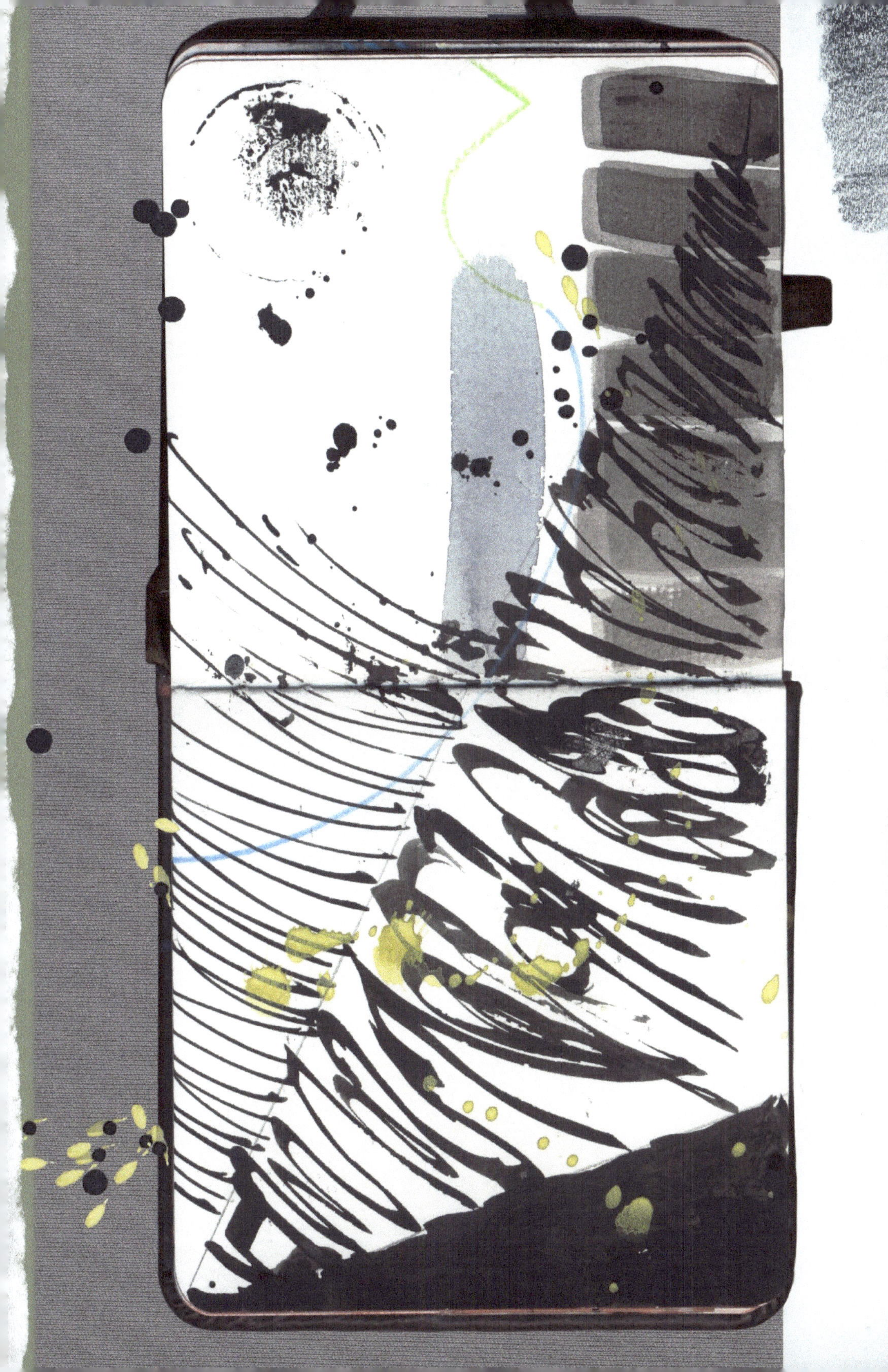

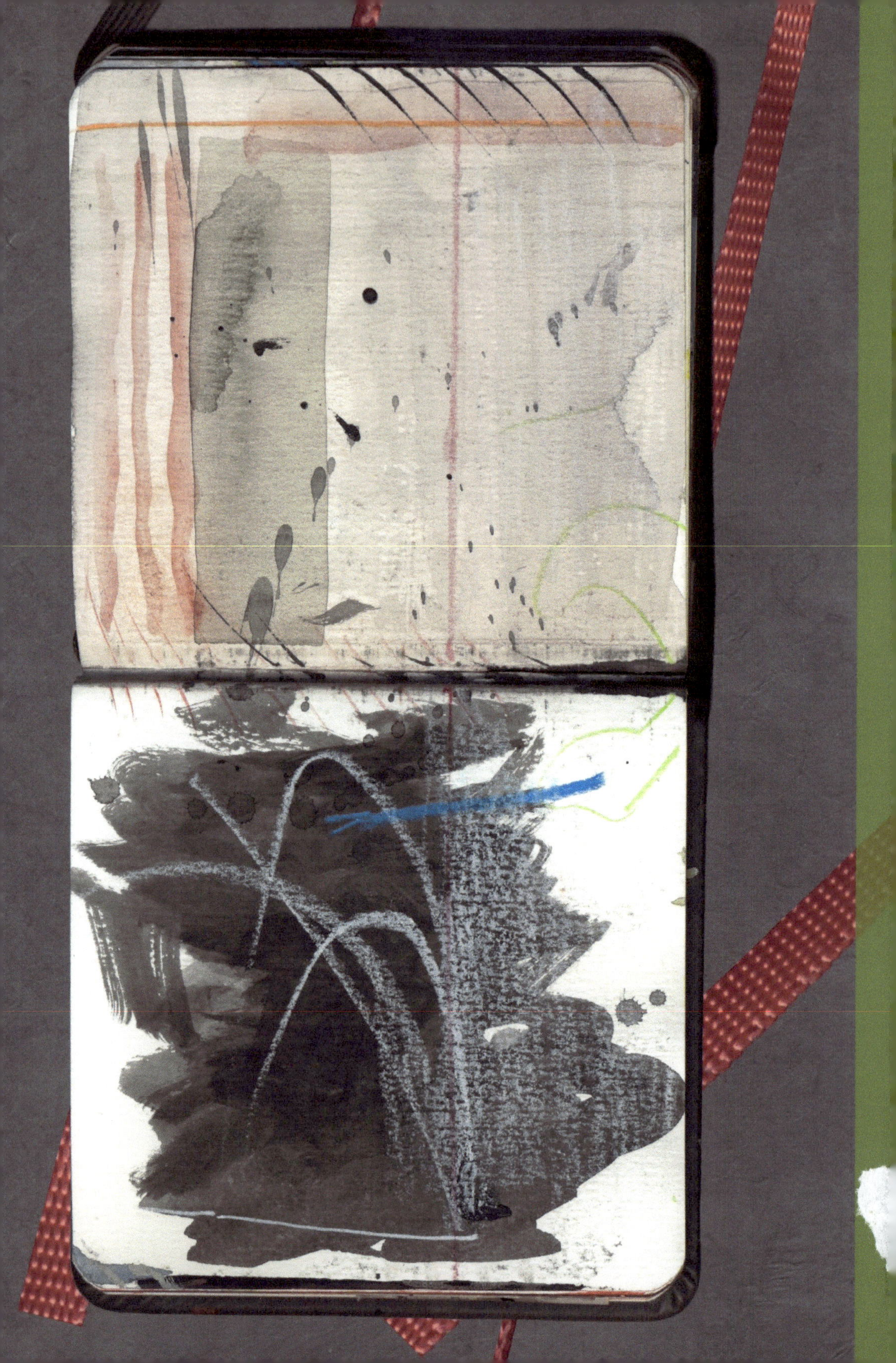

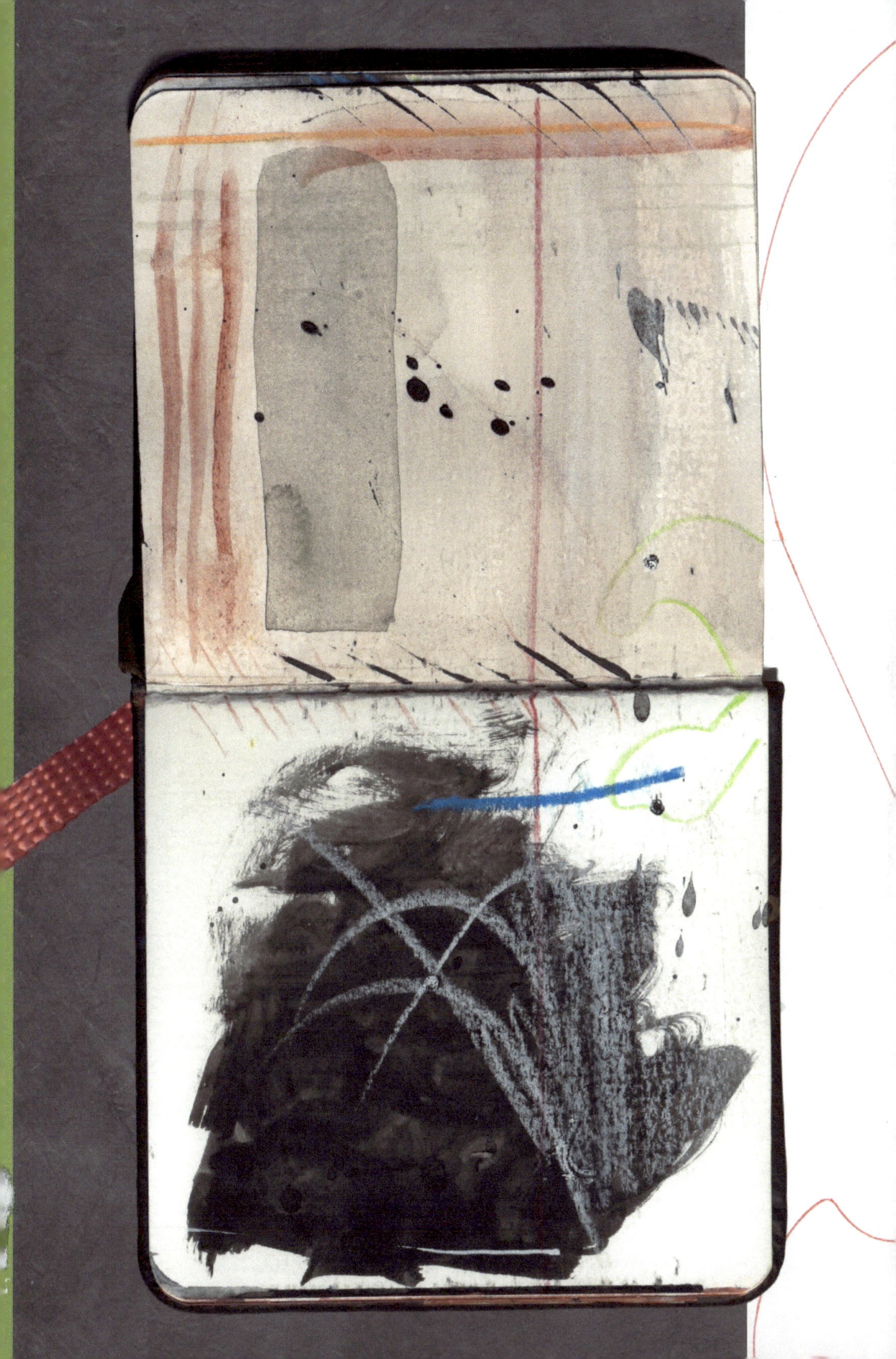

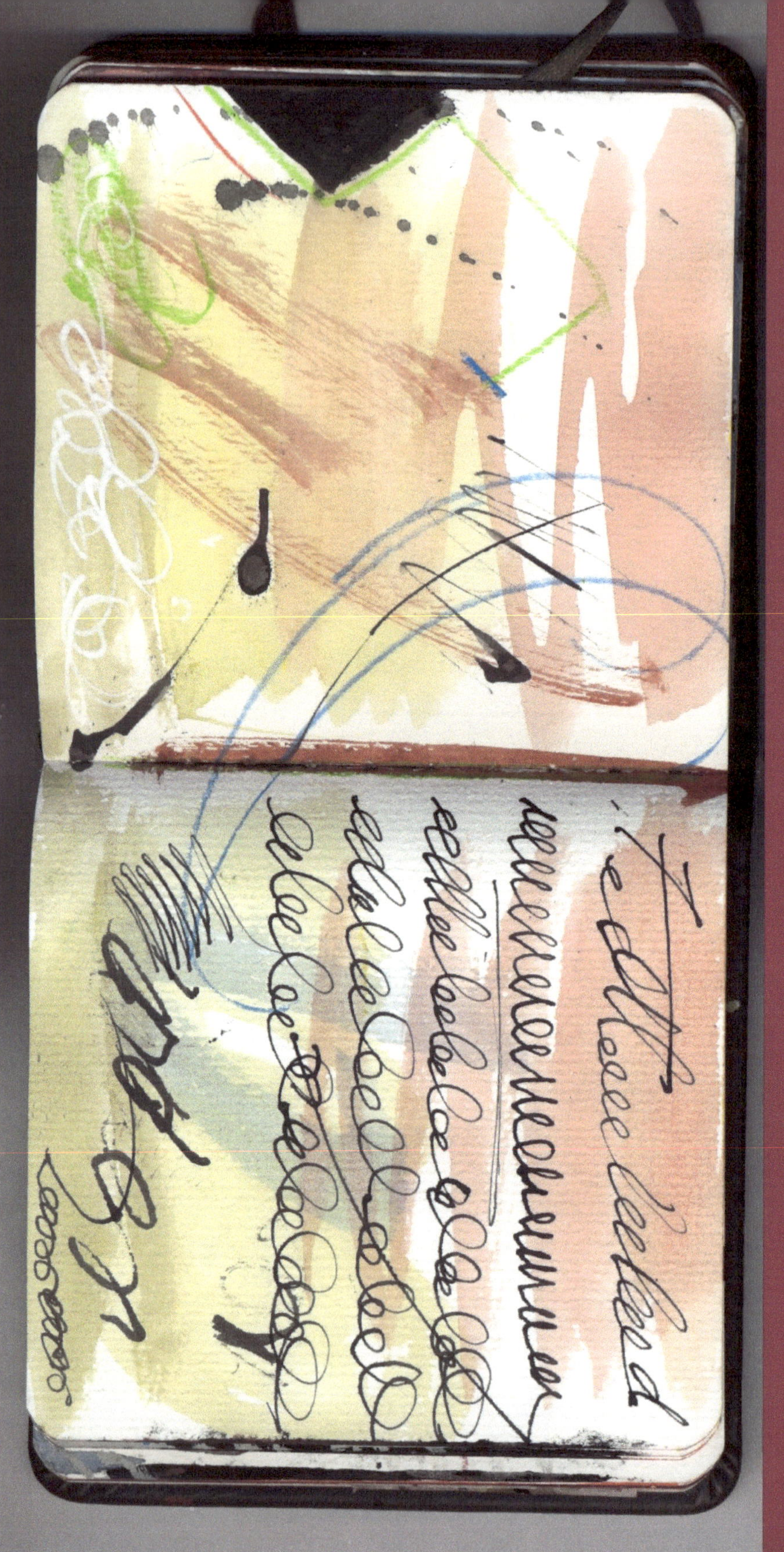

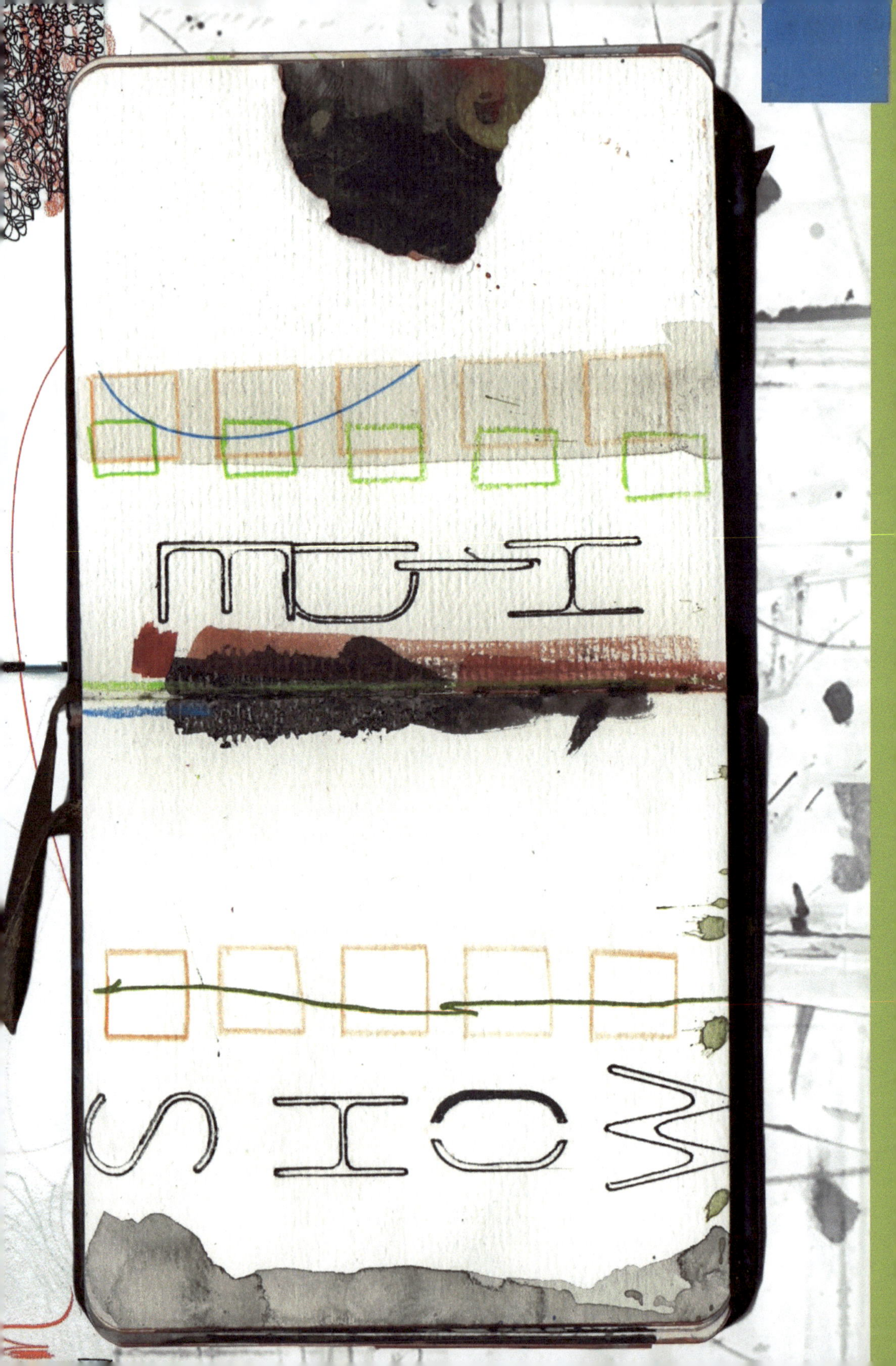

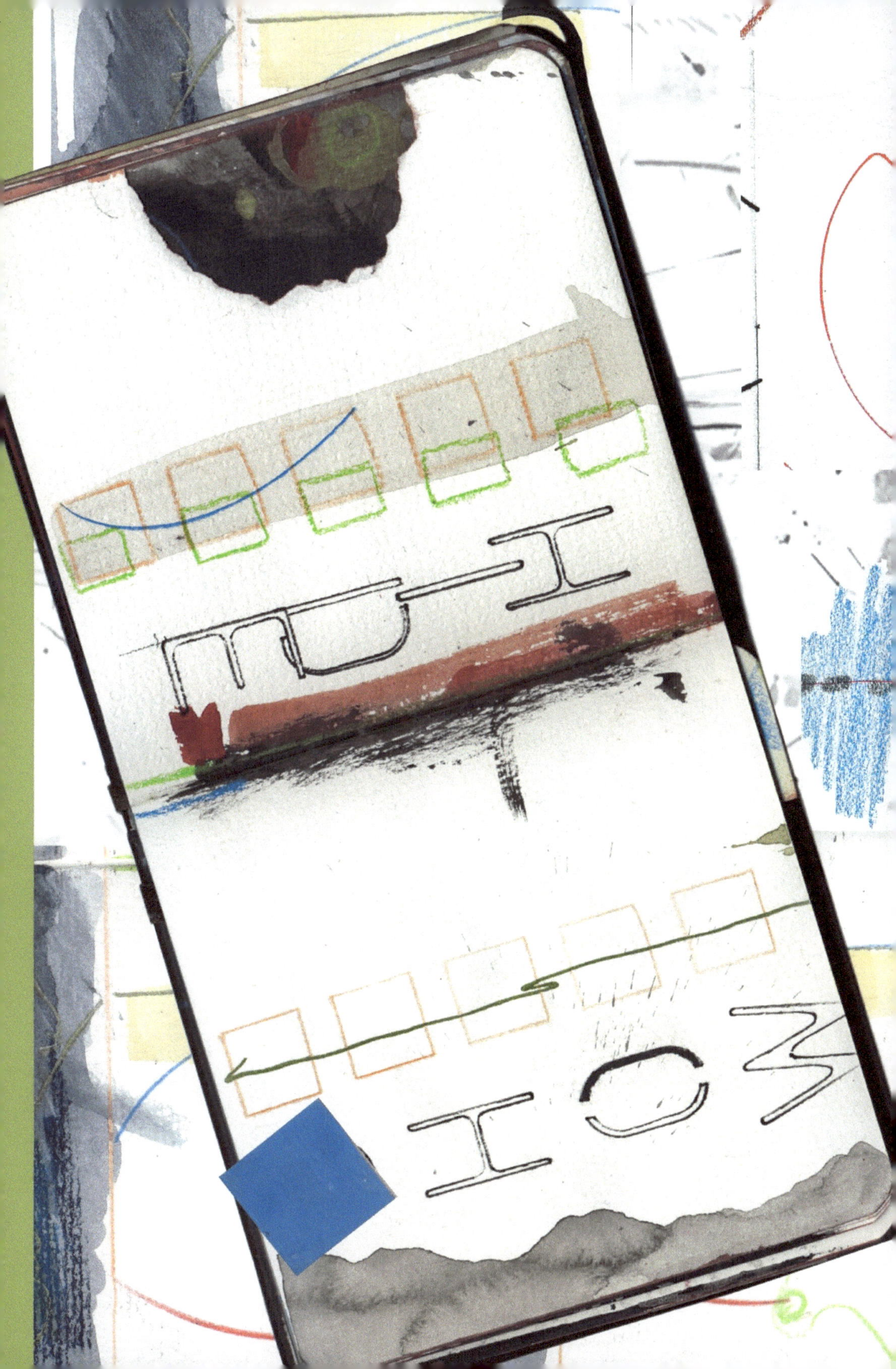

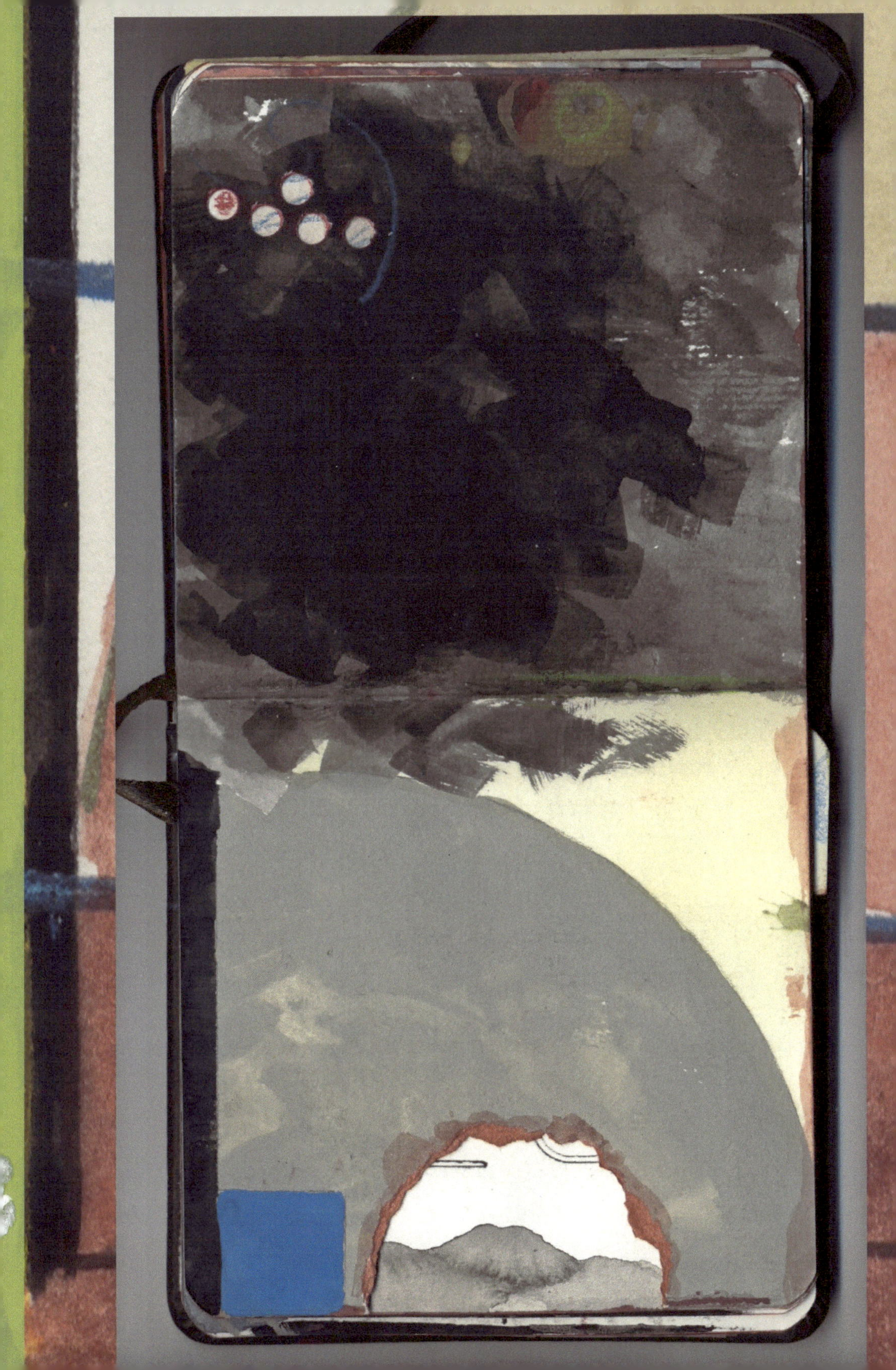

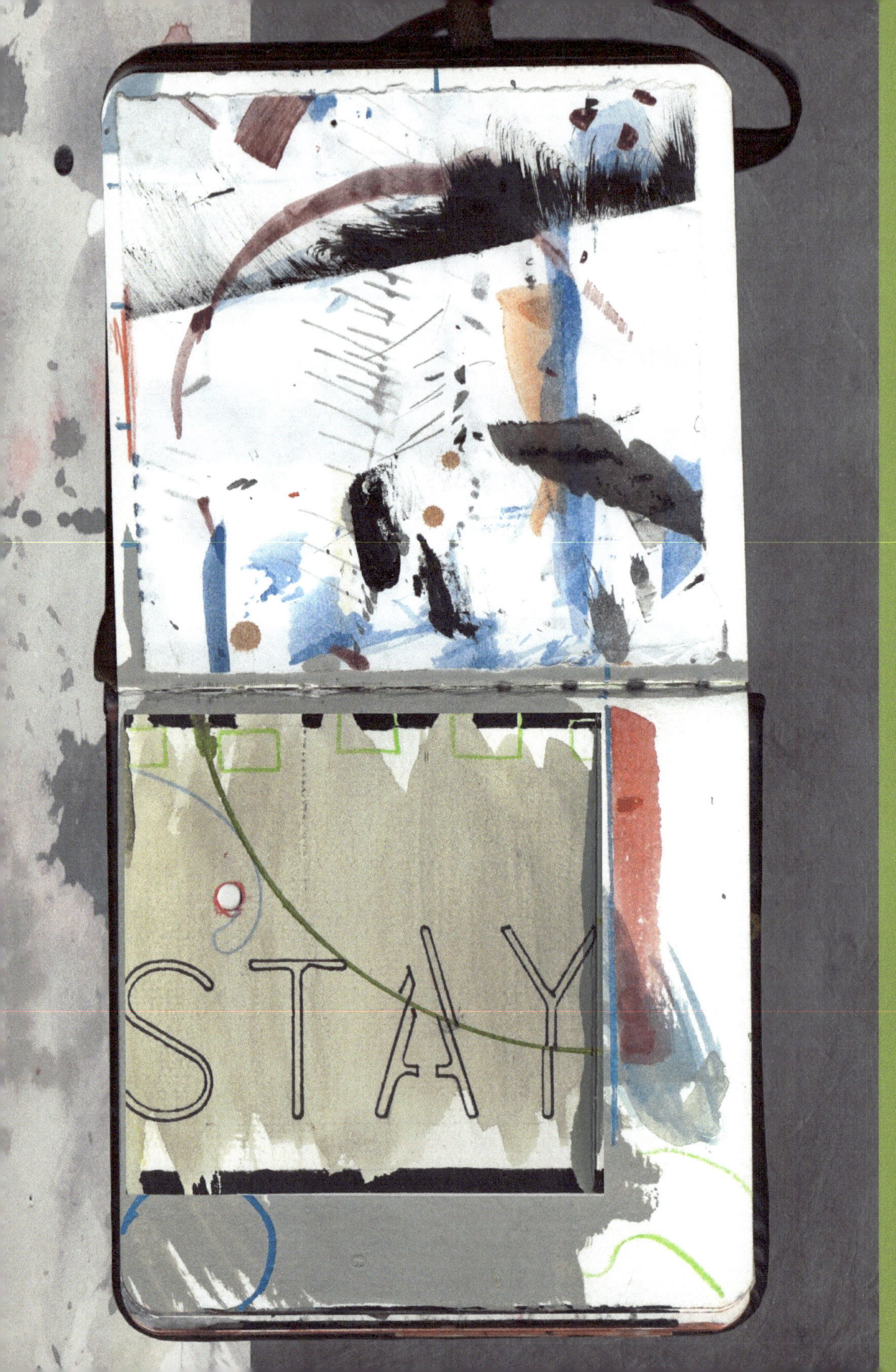
STAY

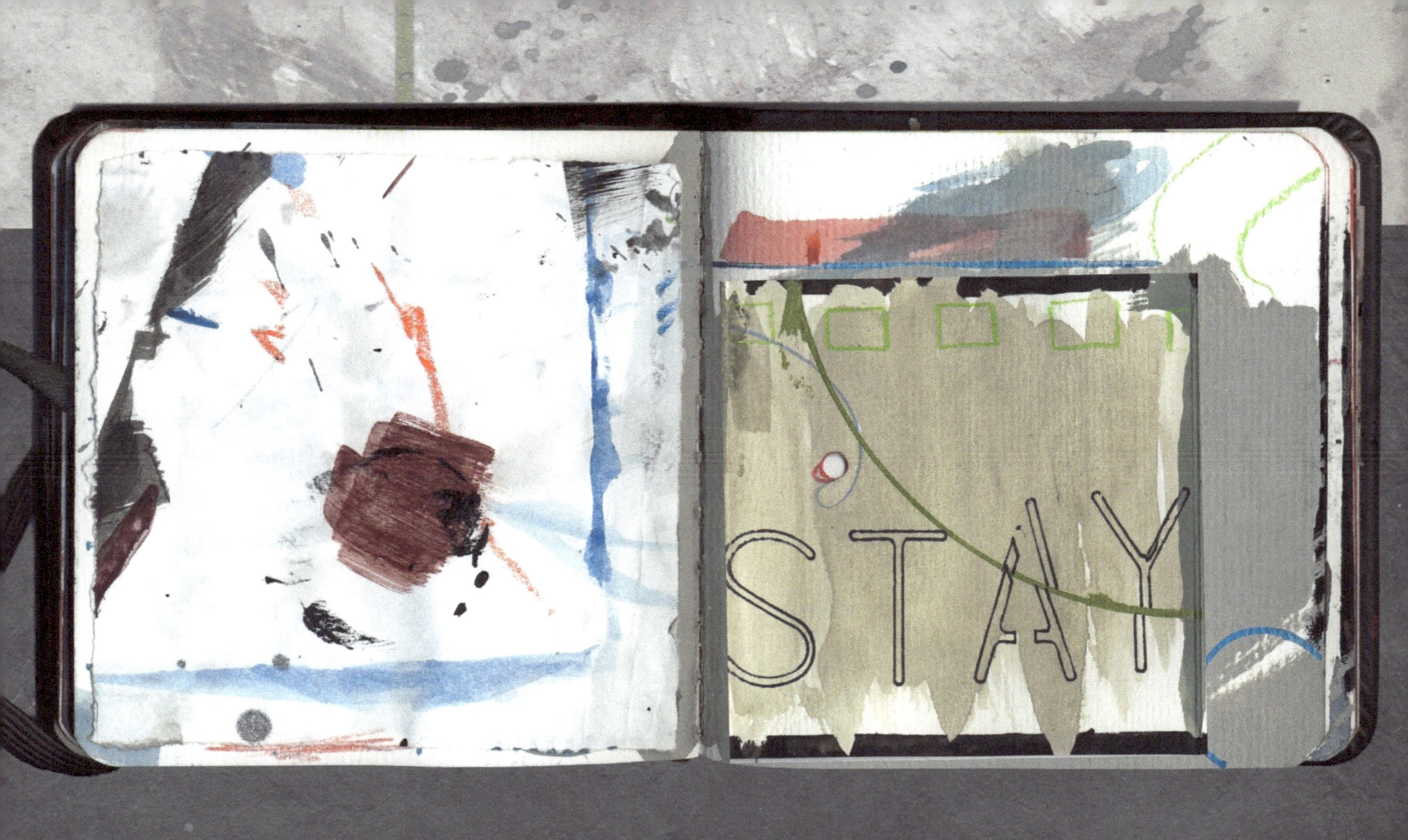
STAY

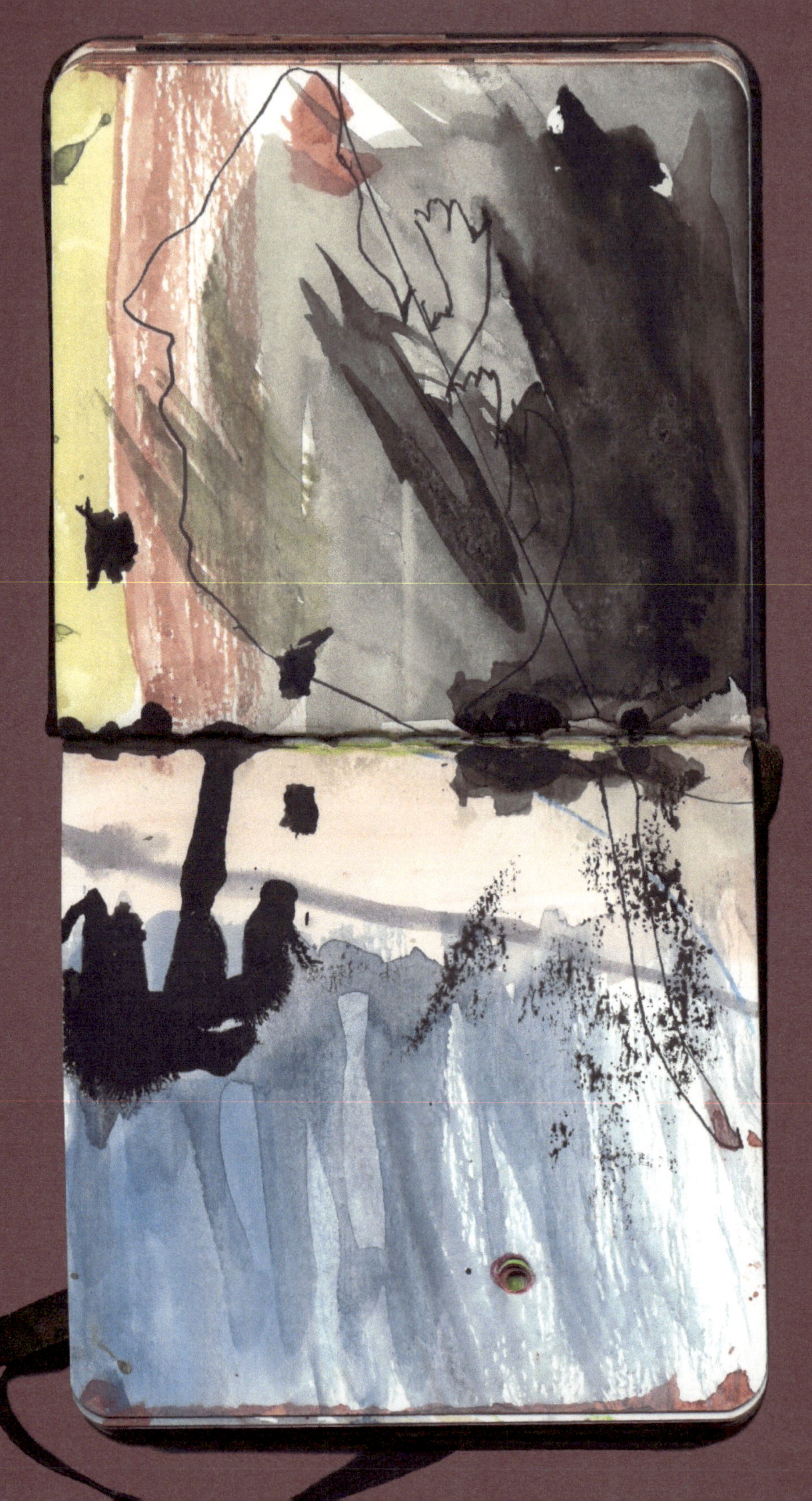

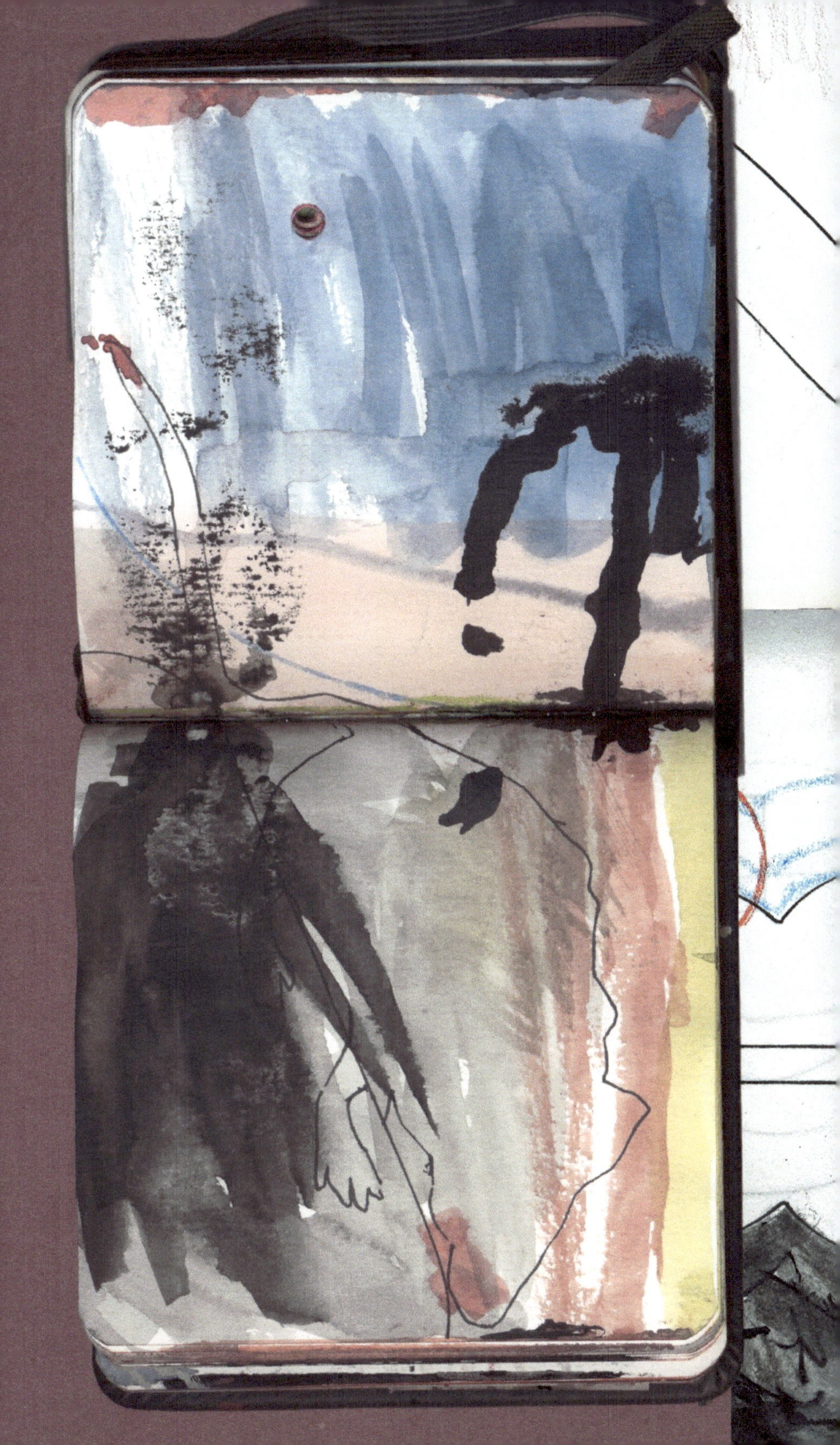

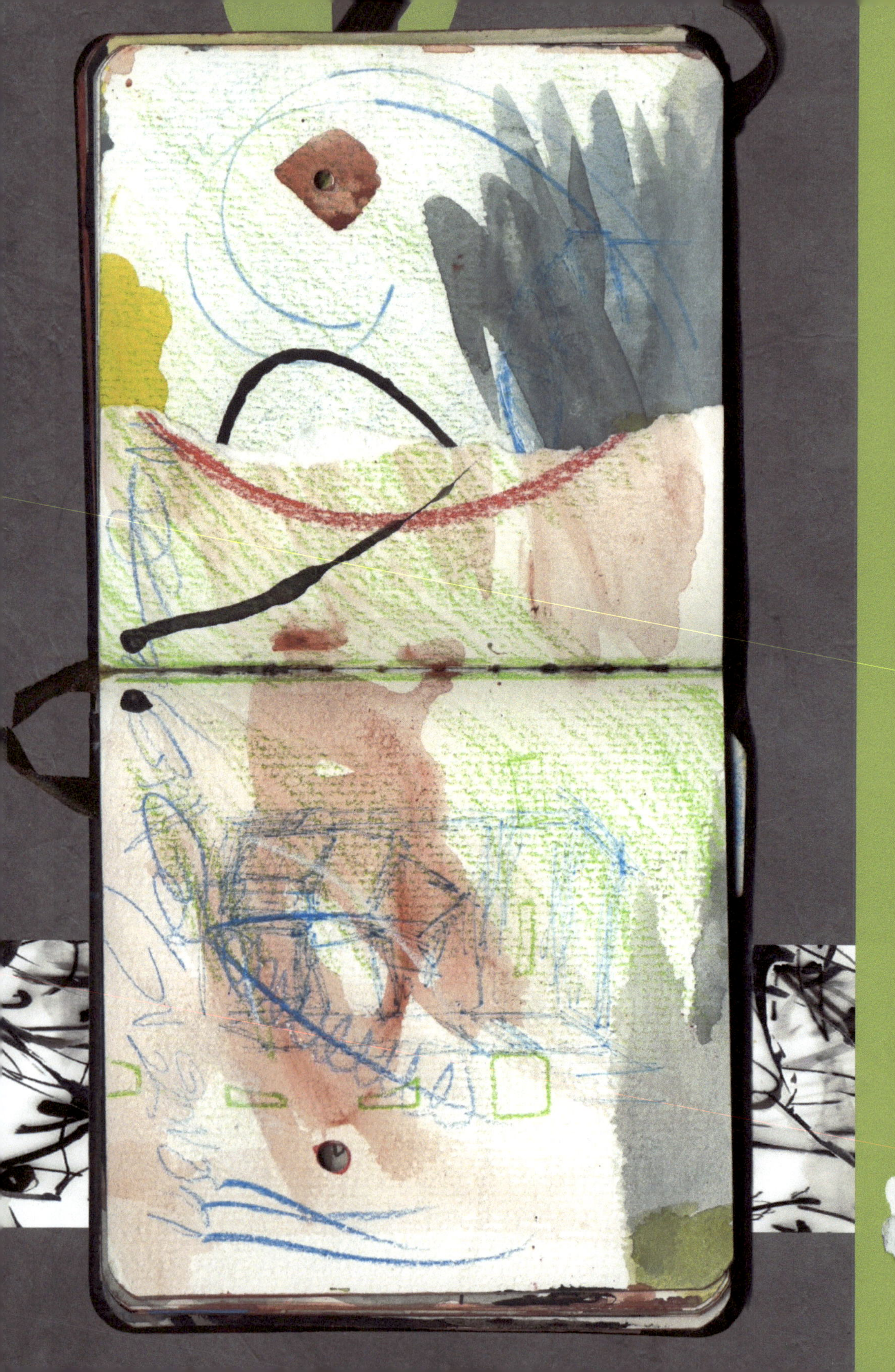

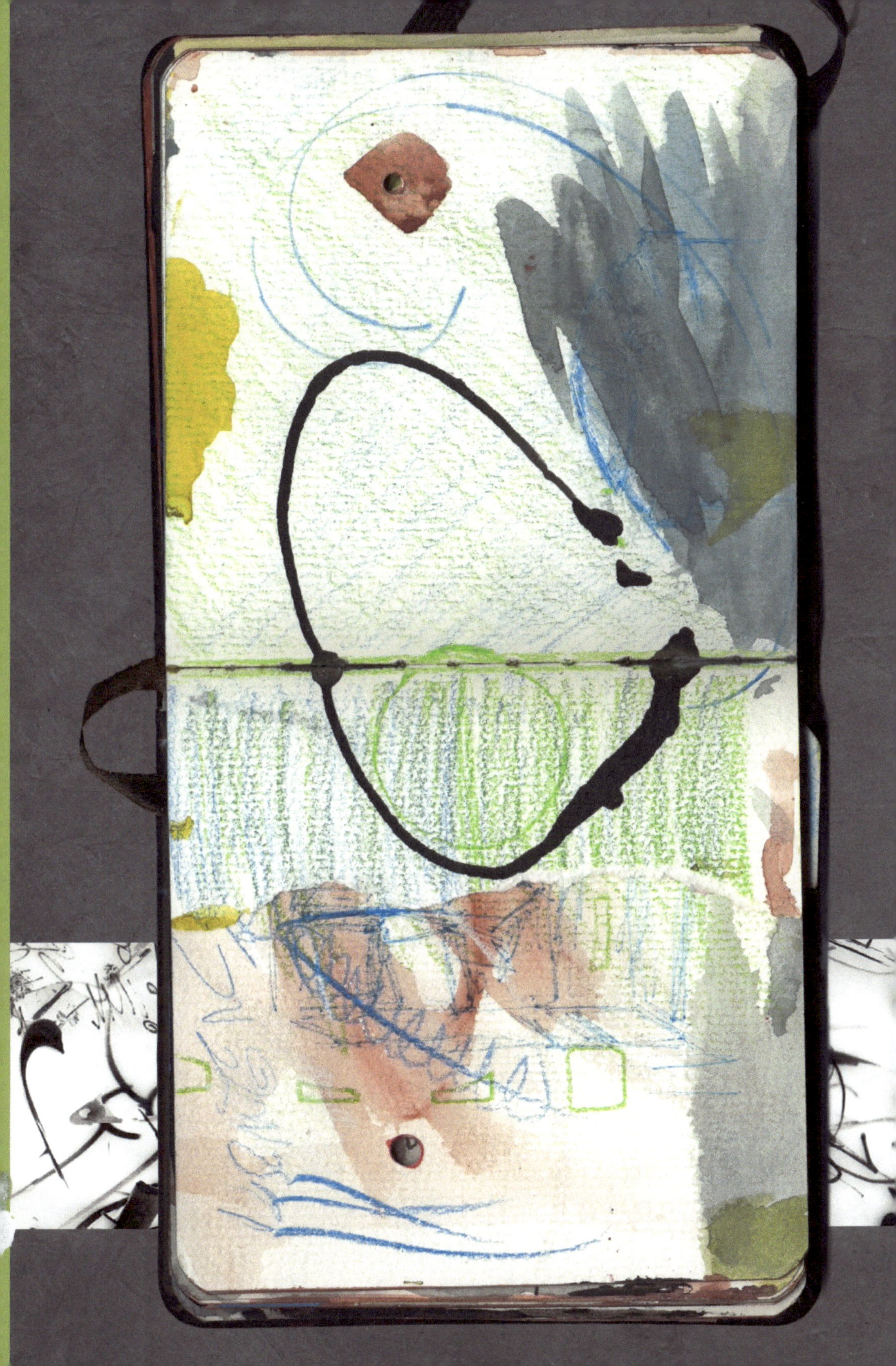

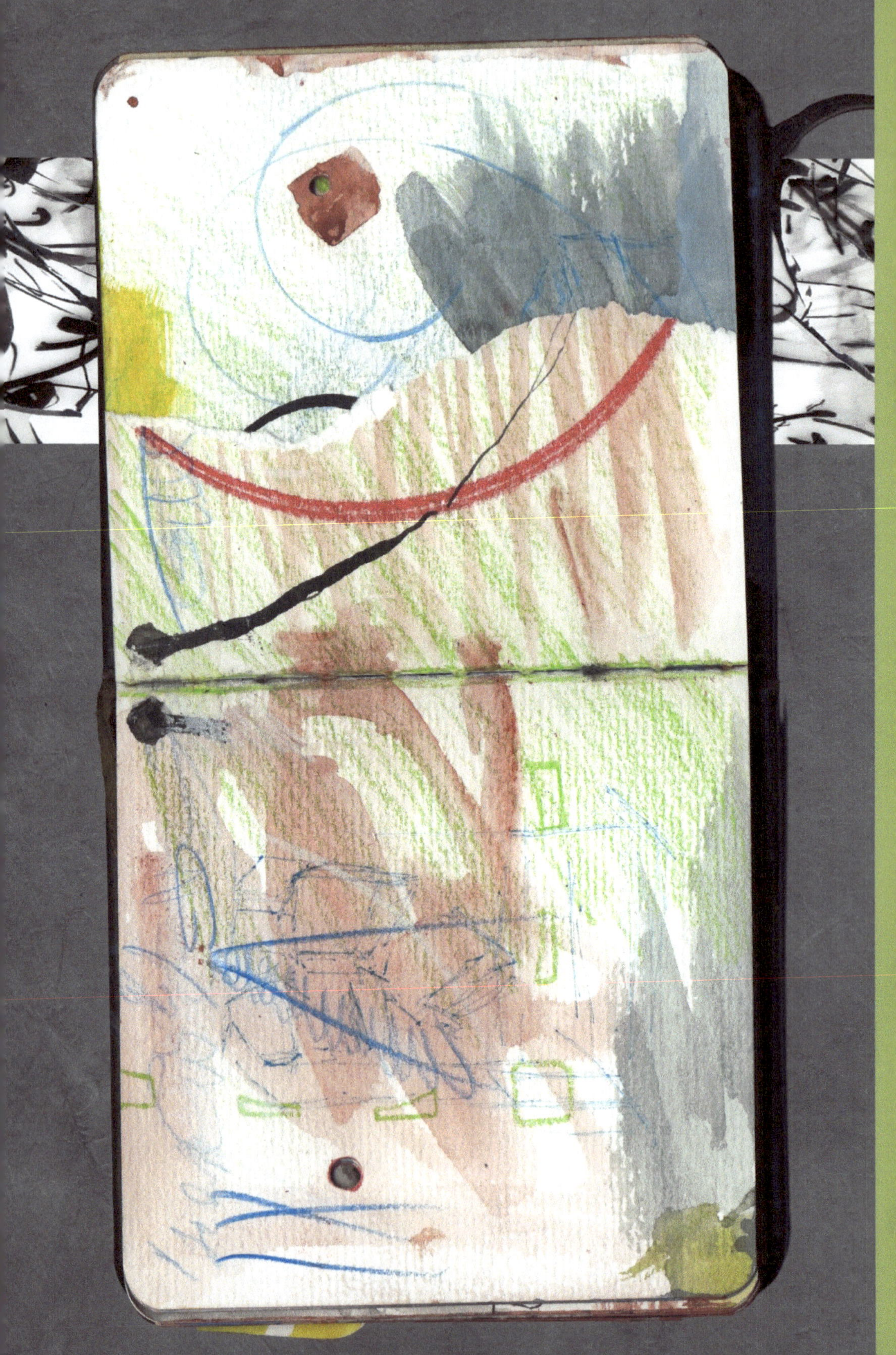

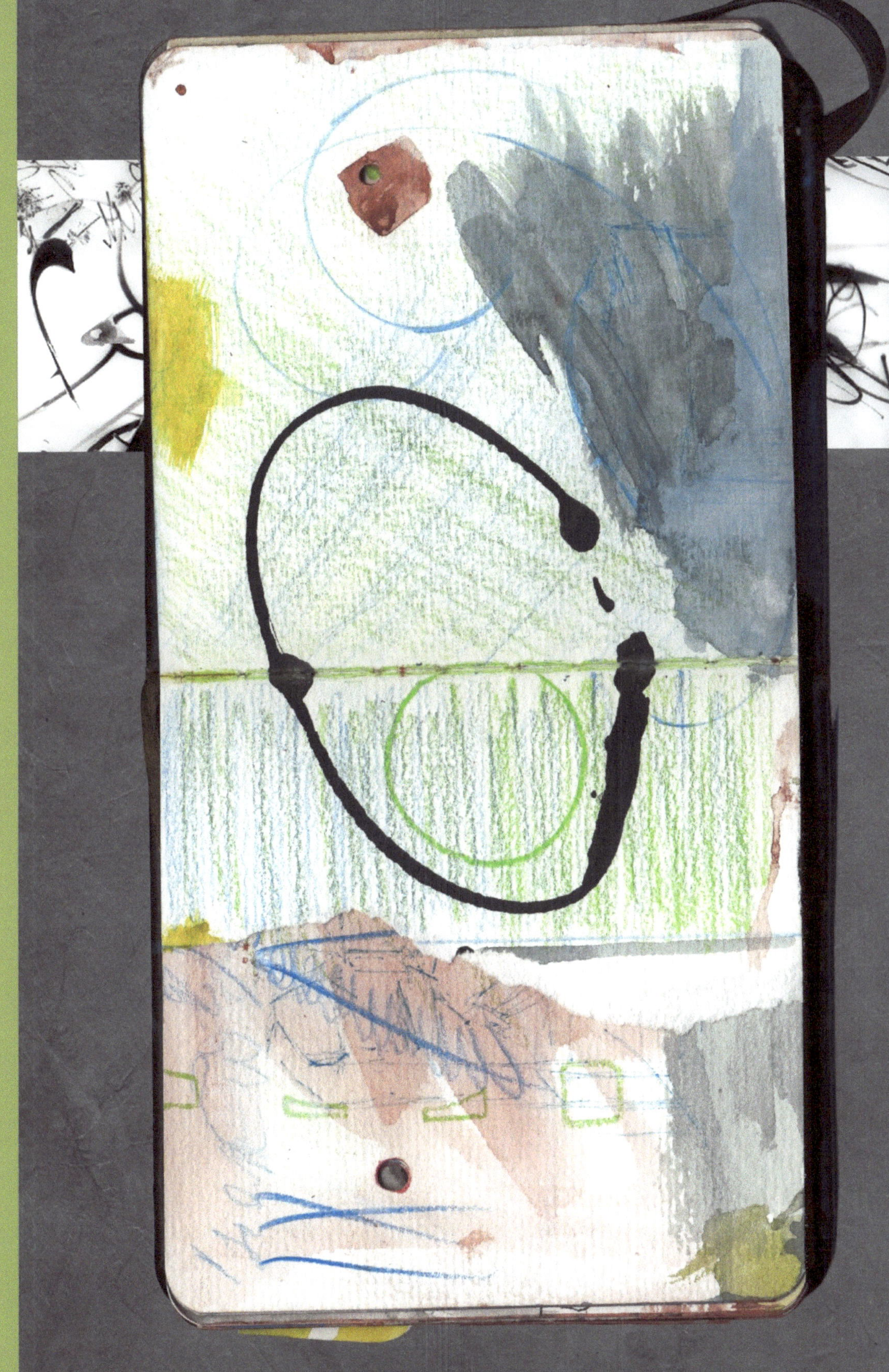

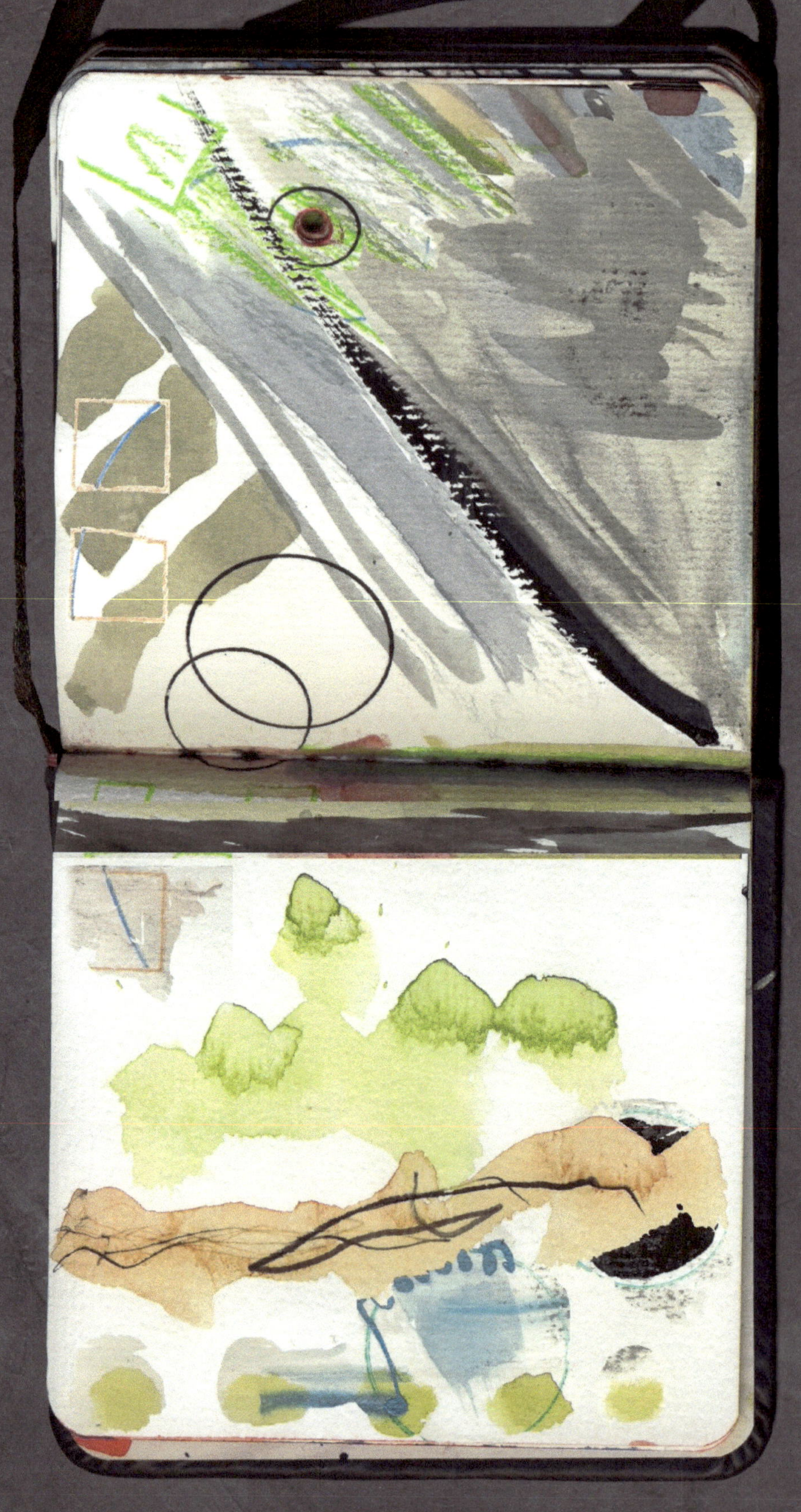

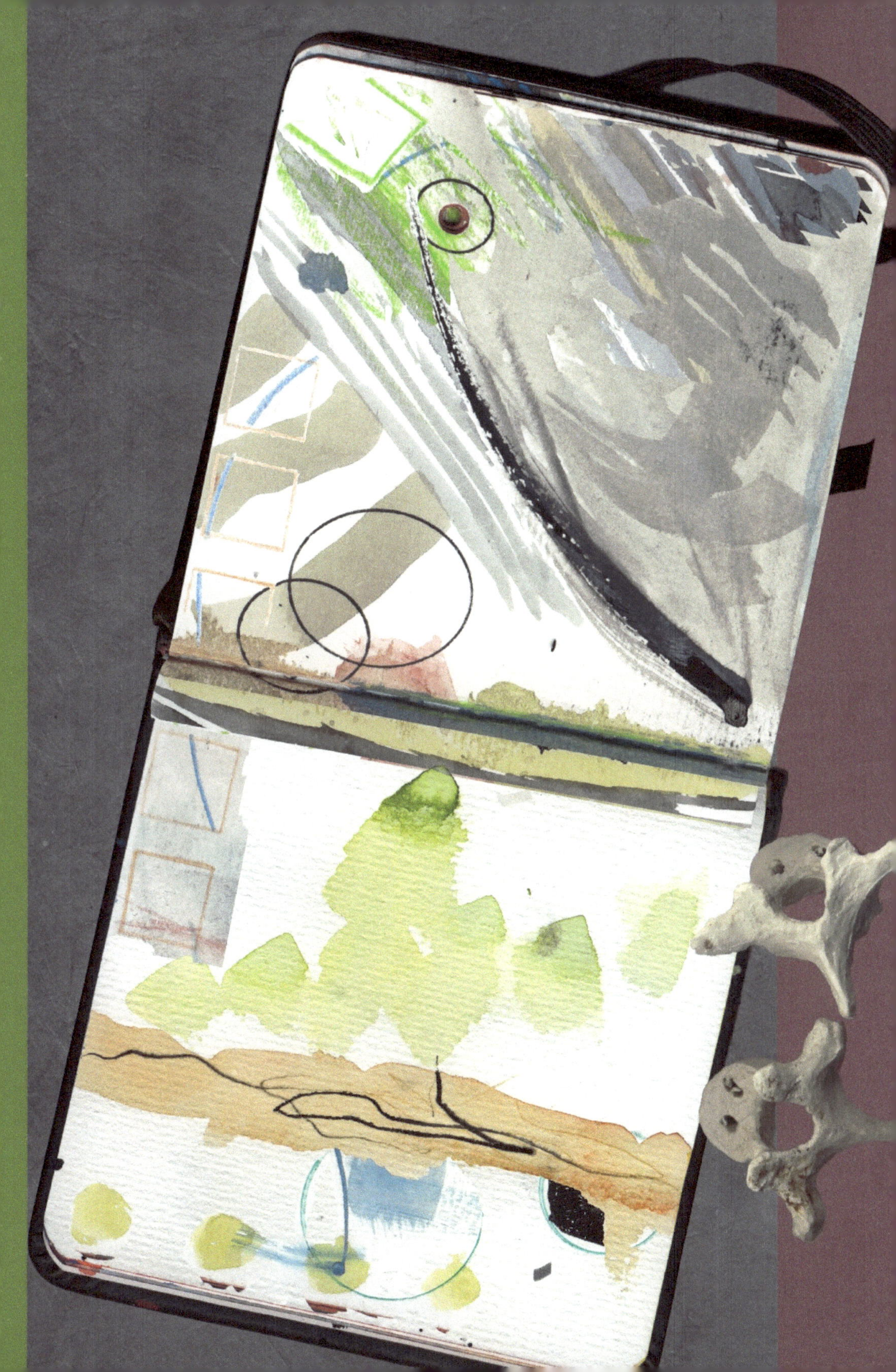

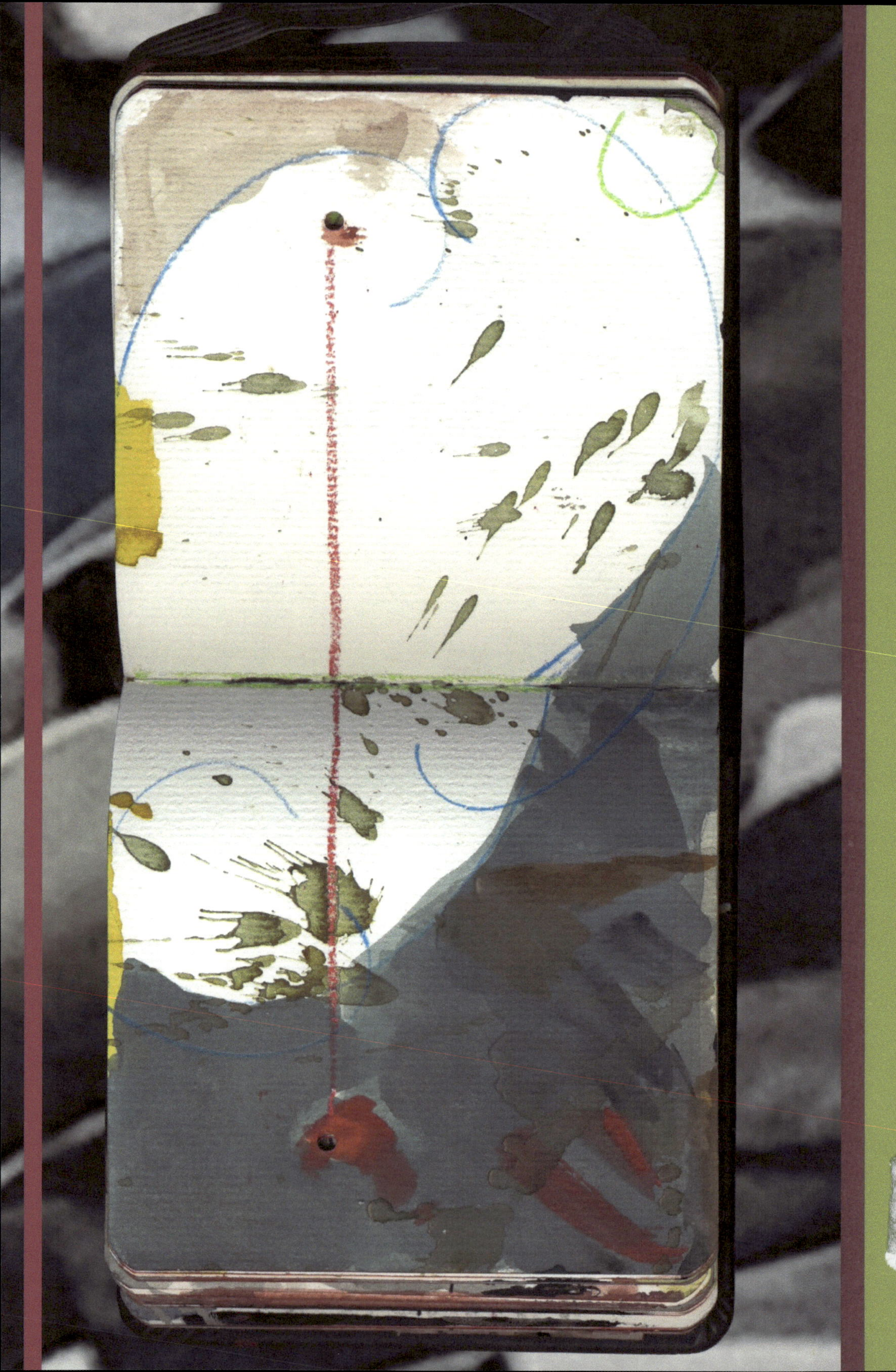

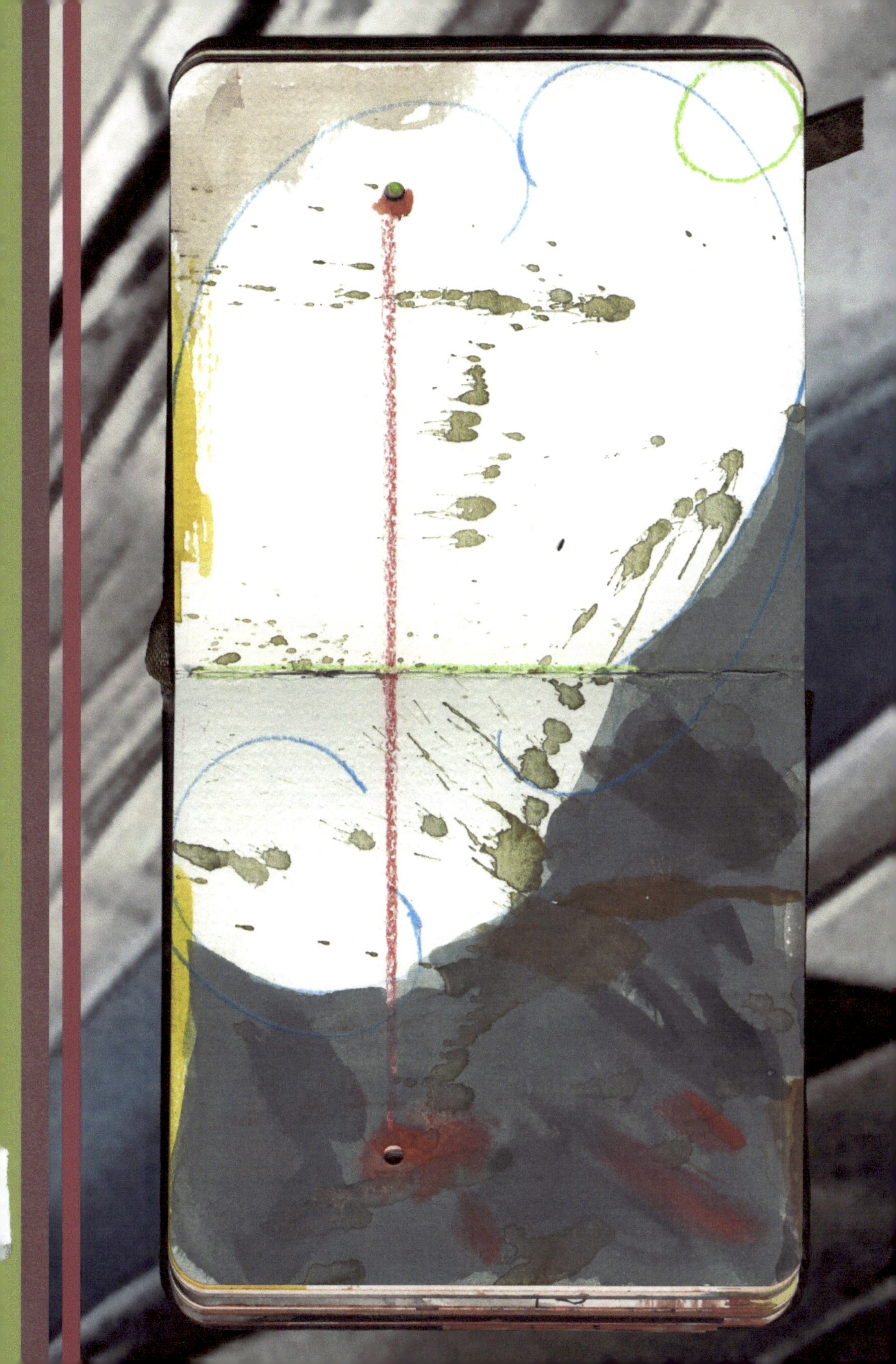

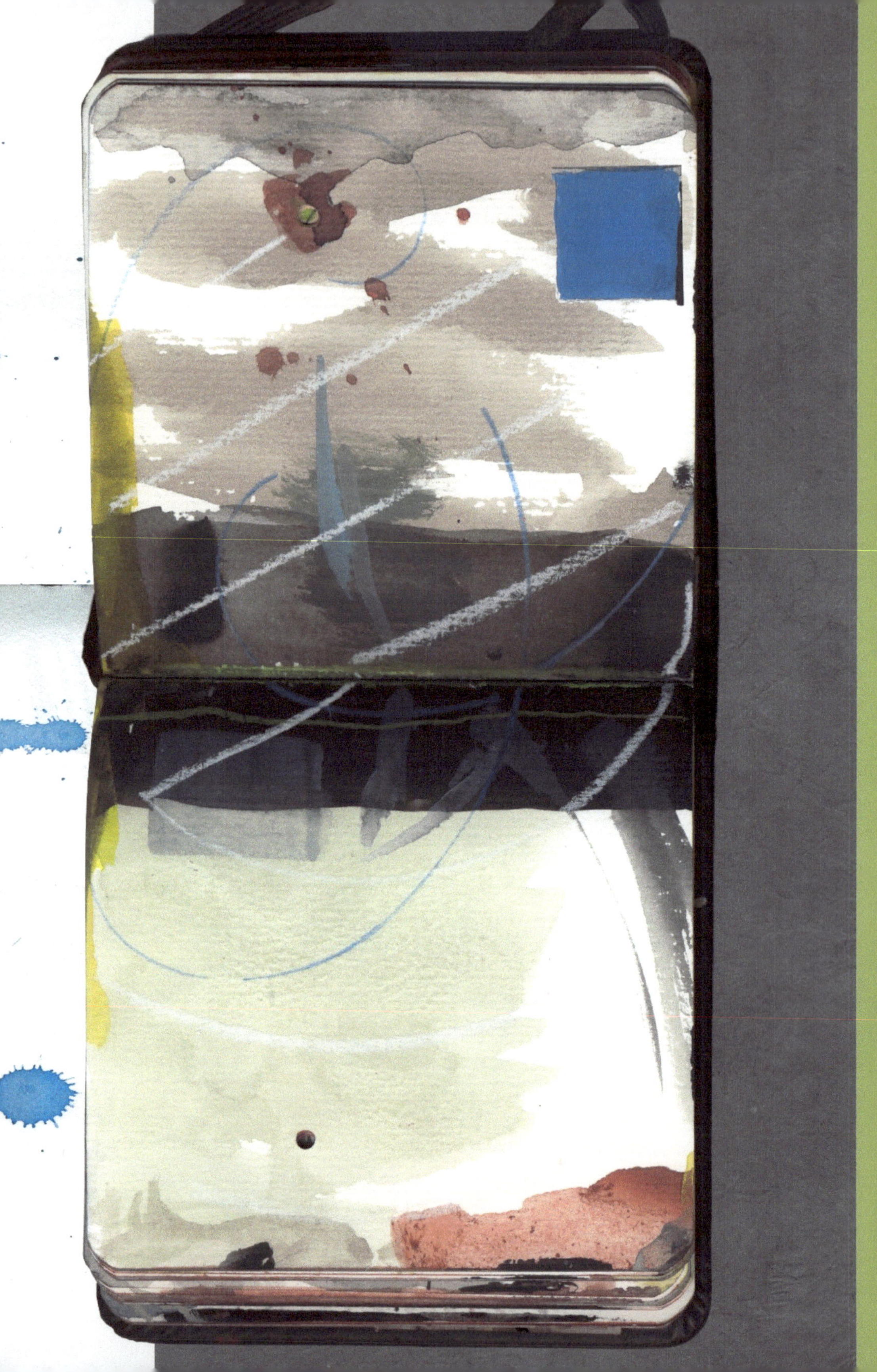

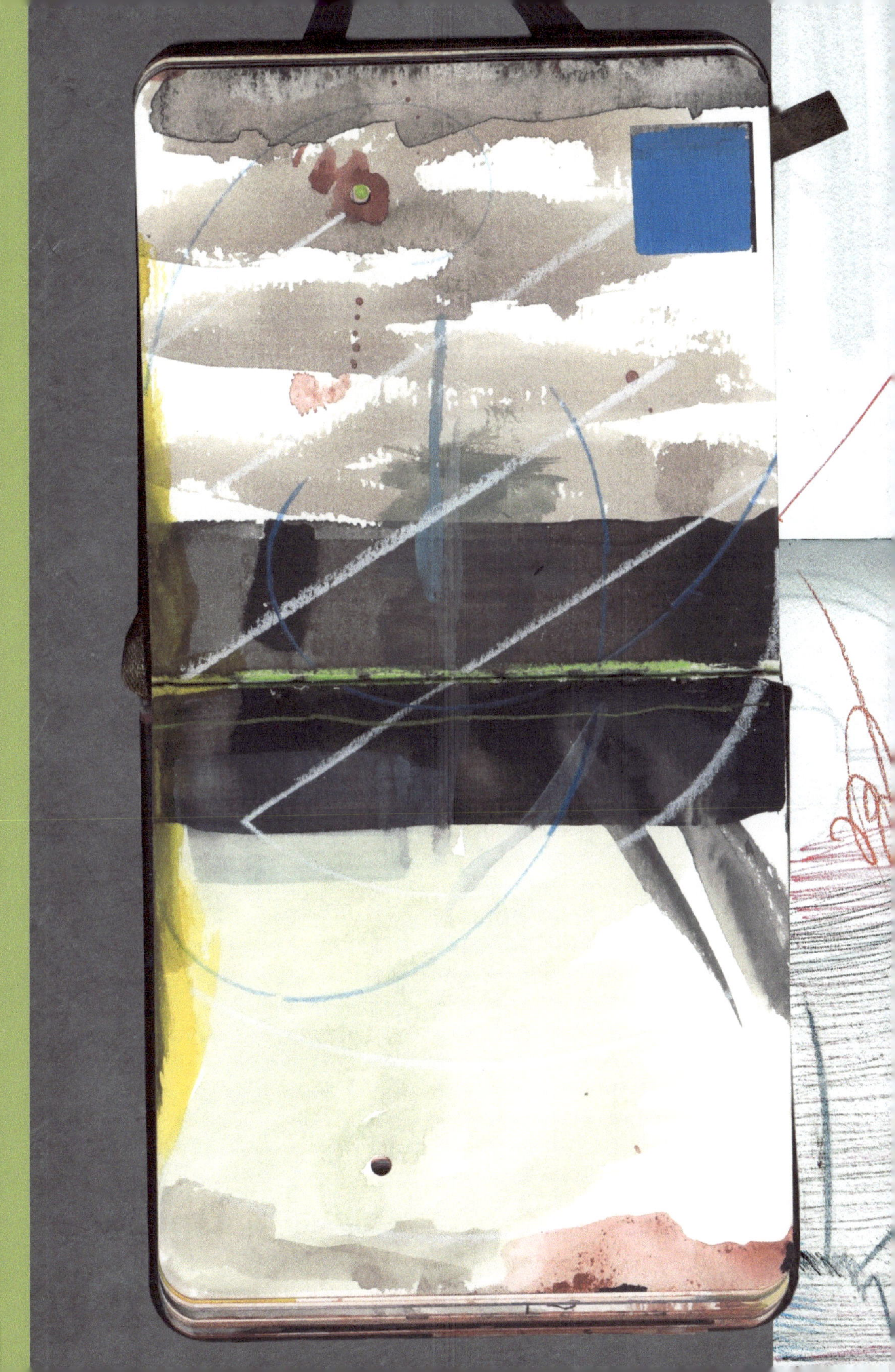

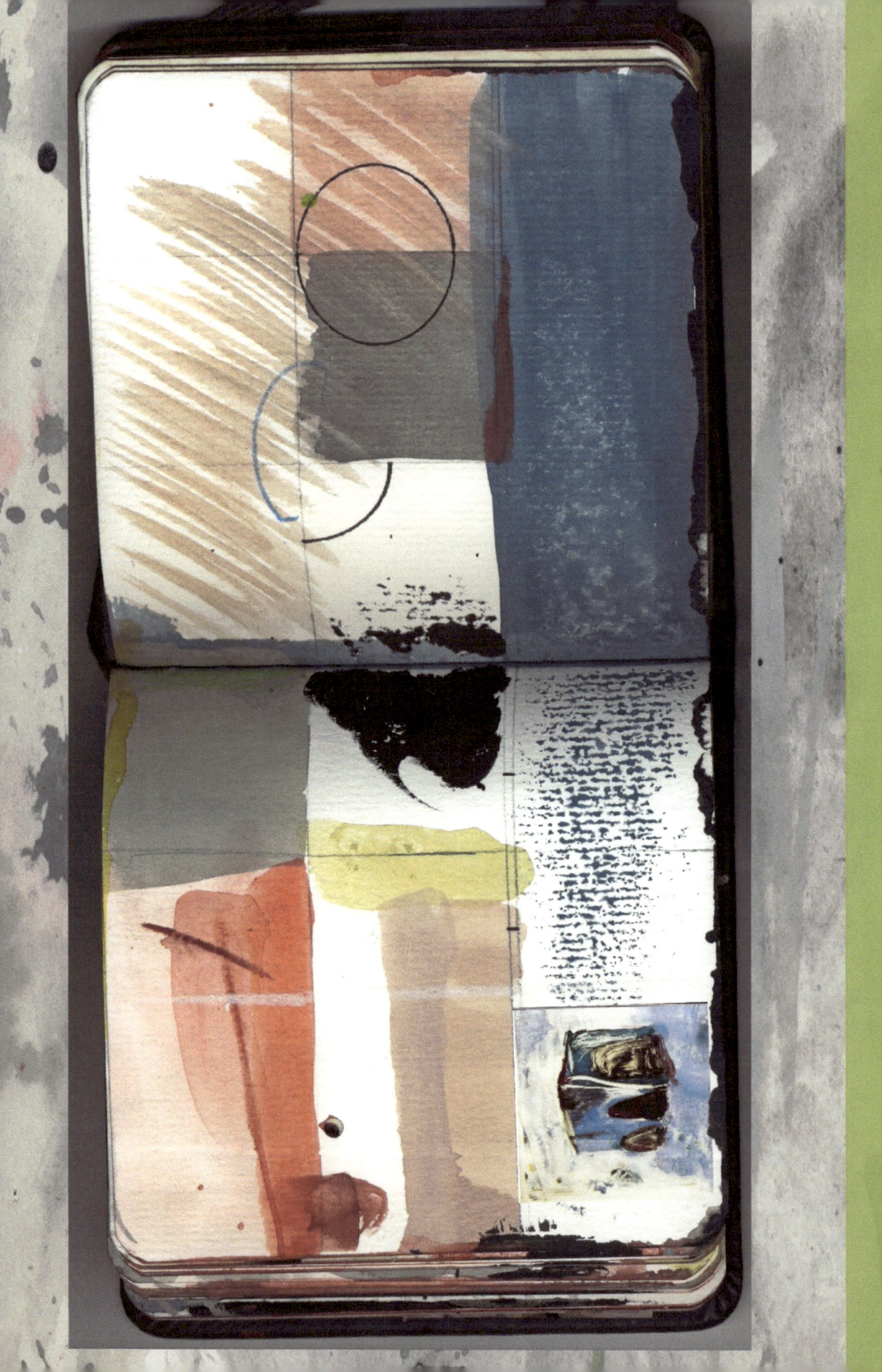

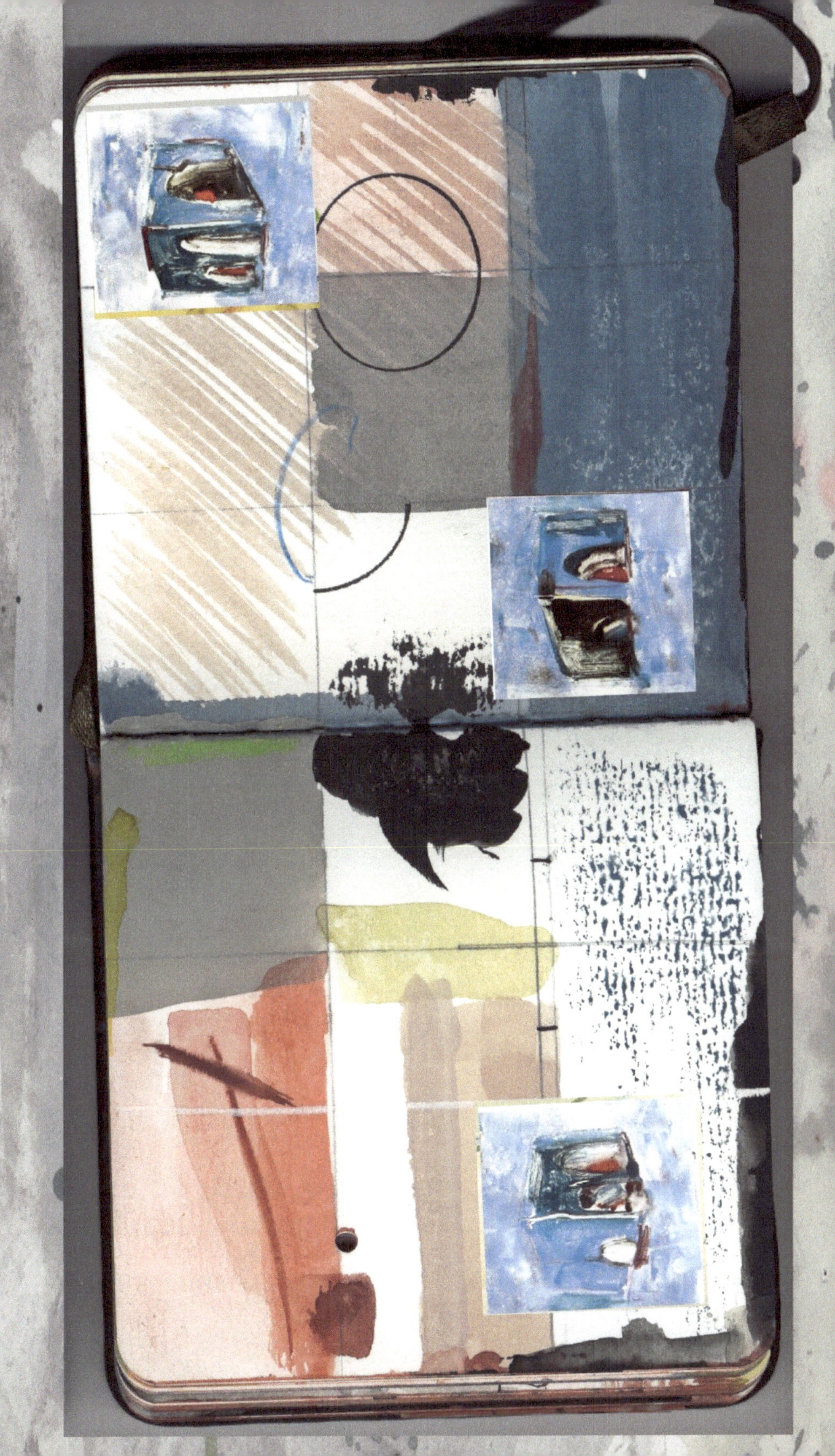

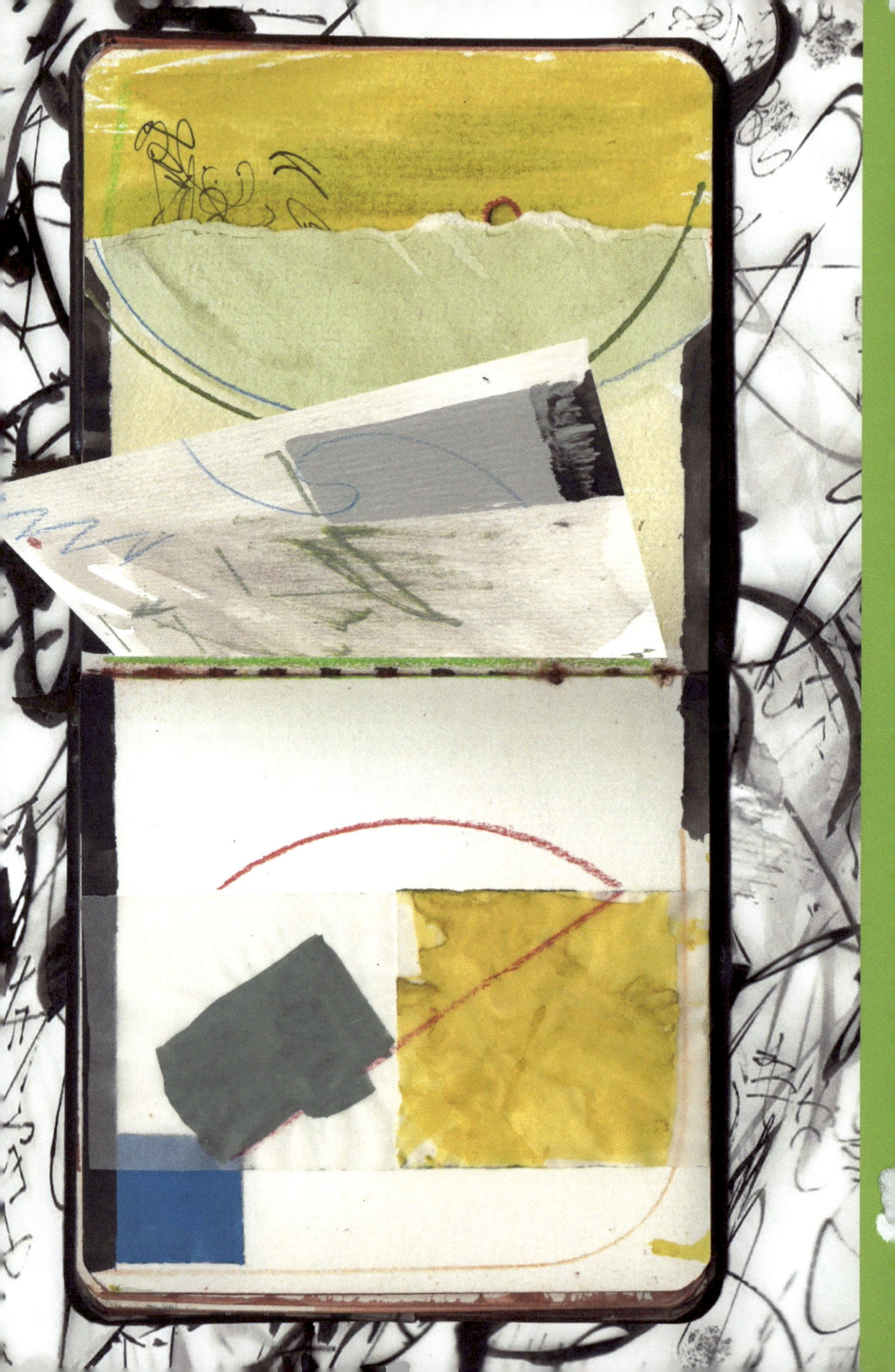

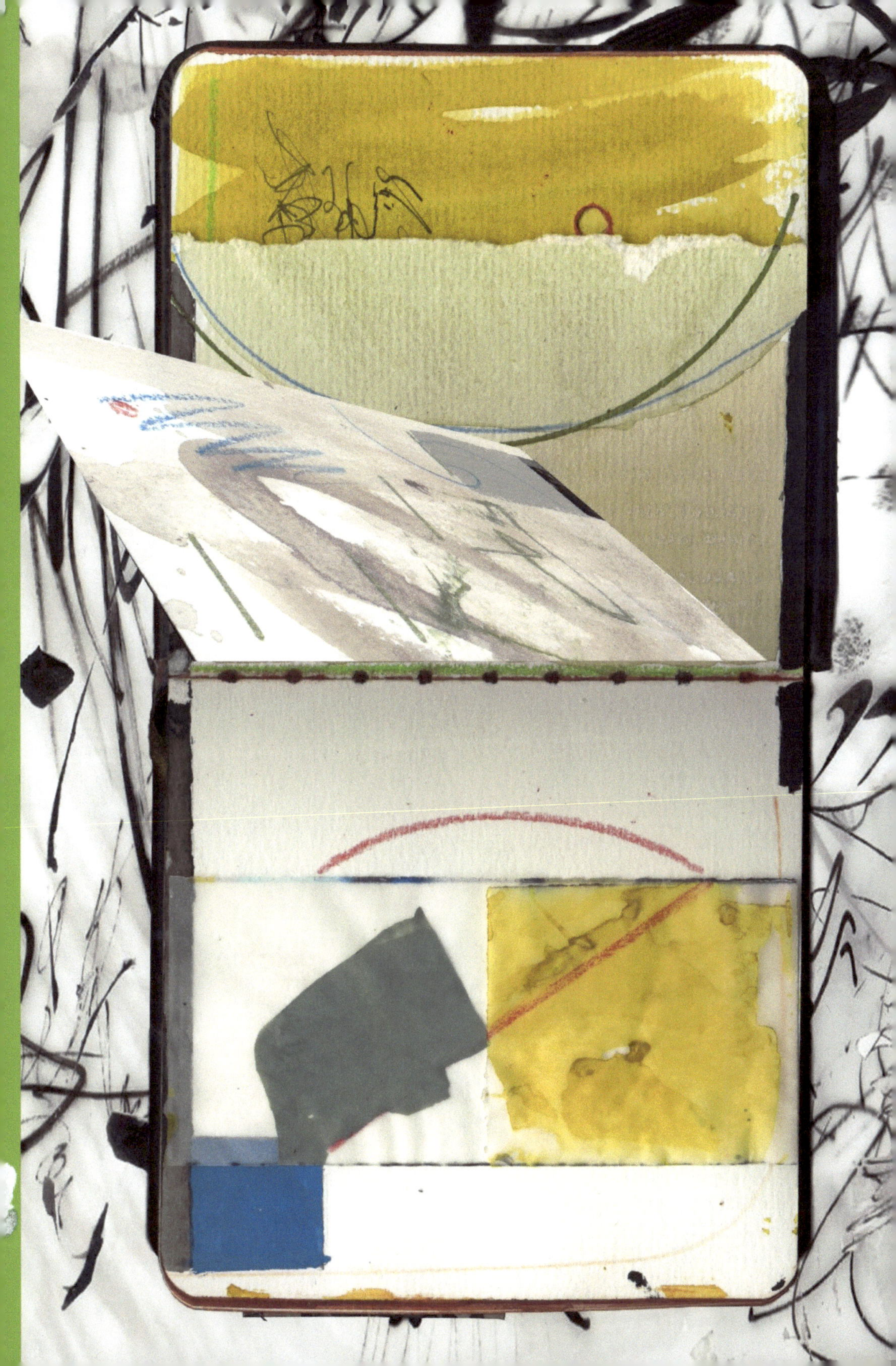

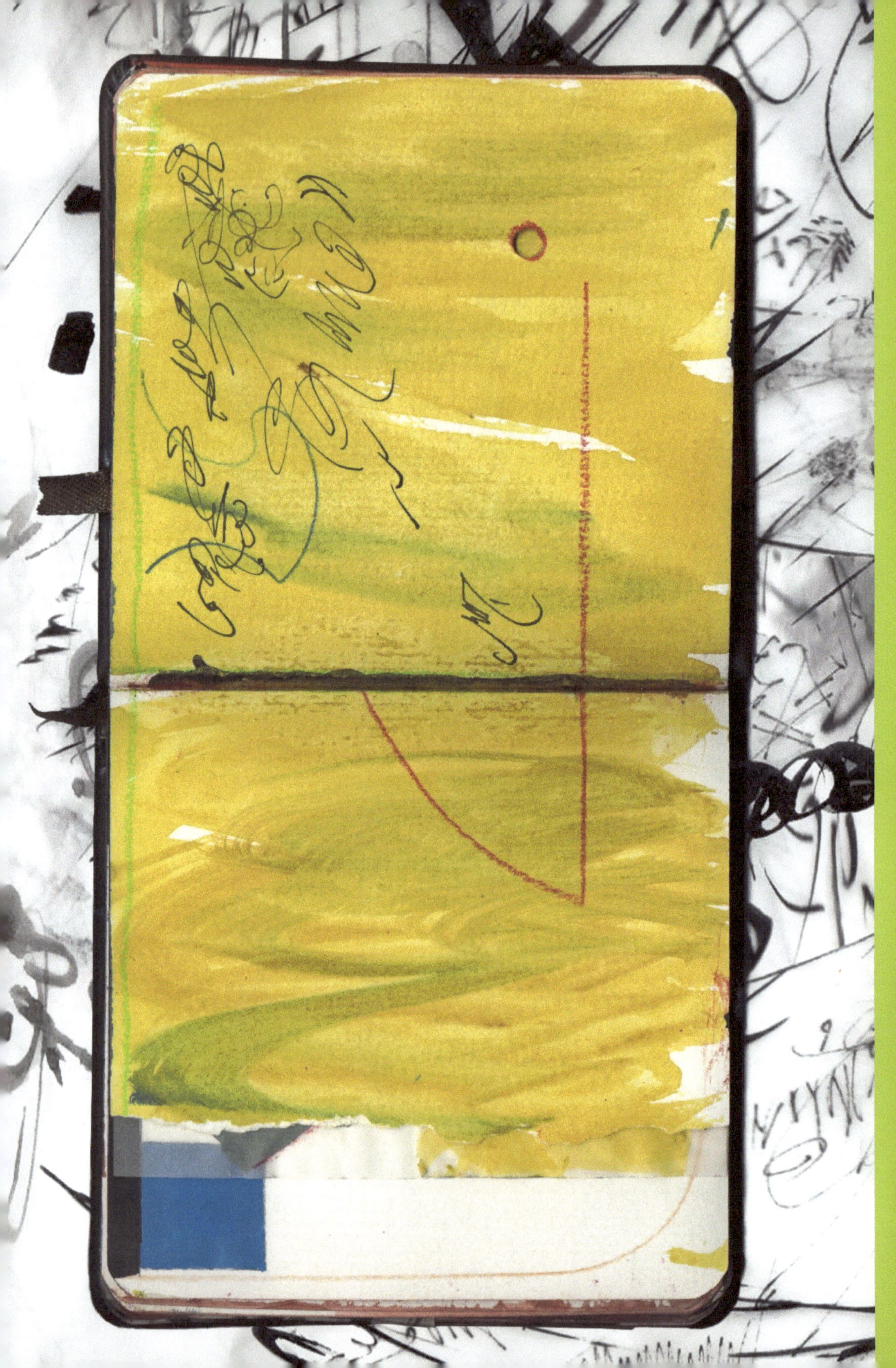

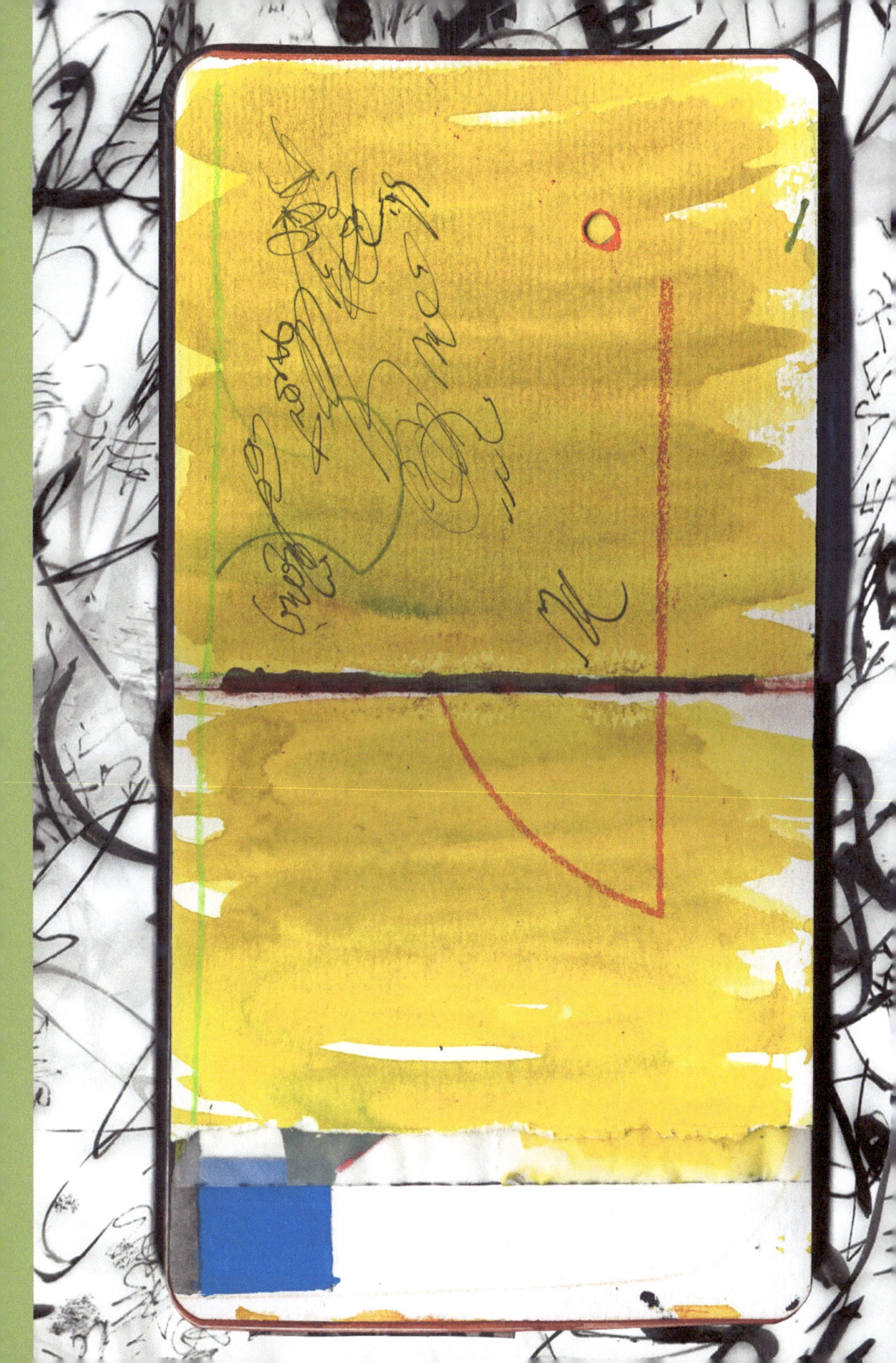

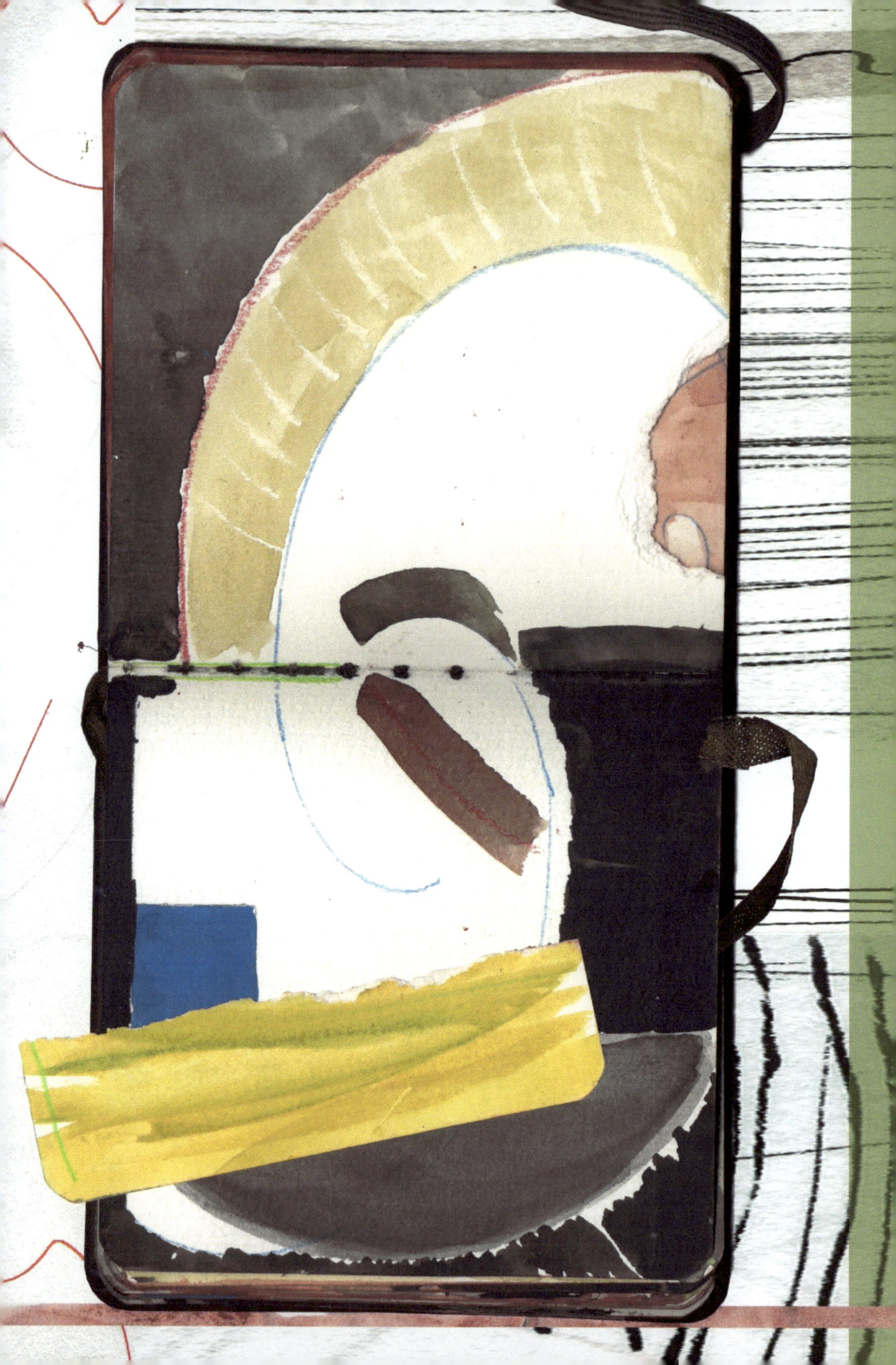

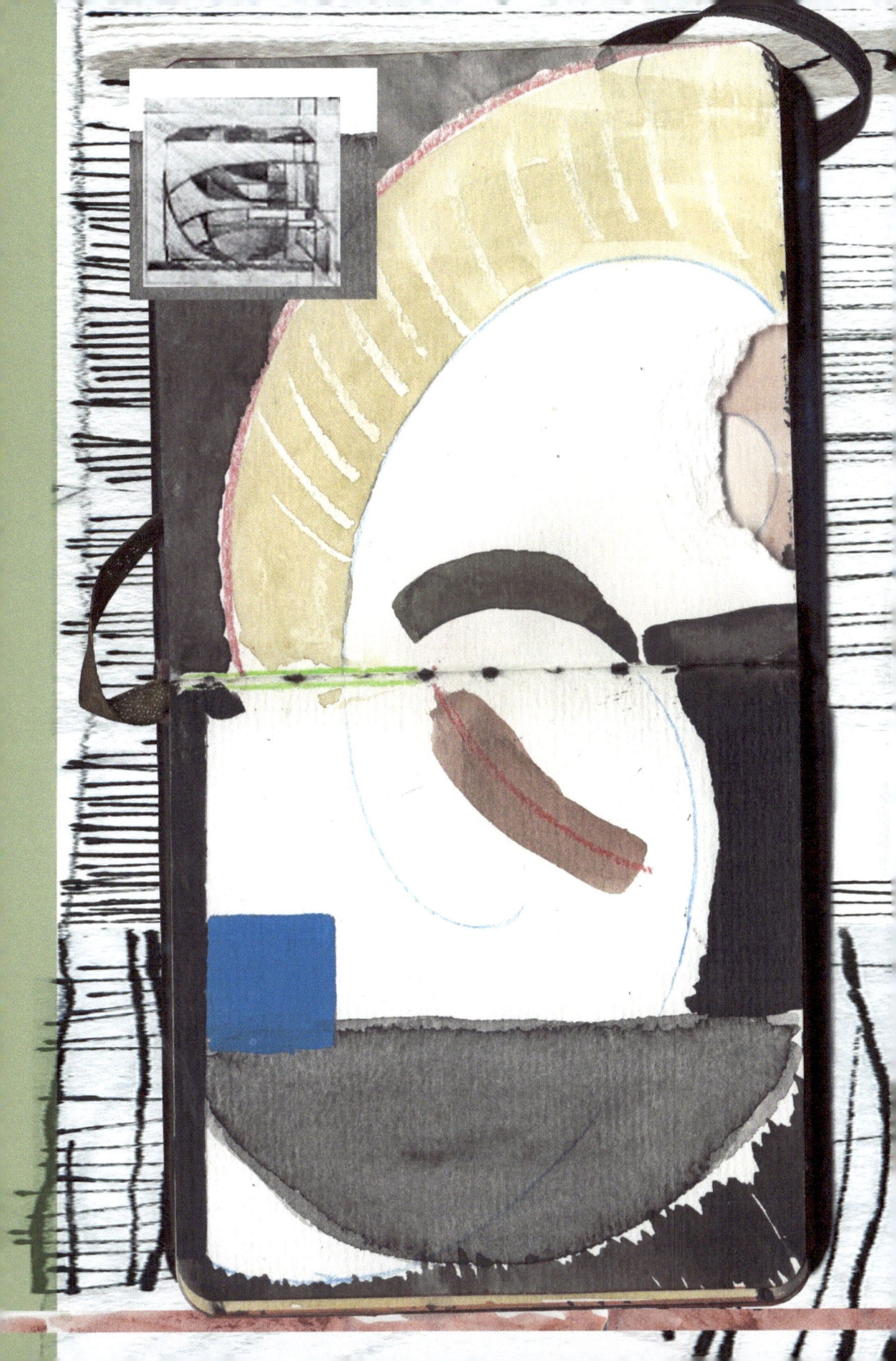

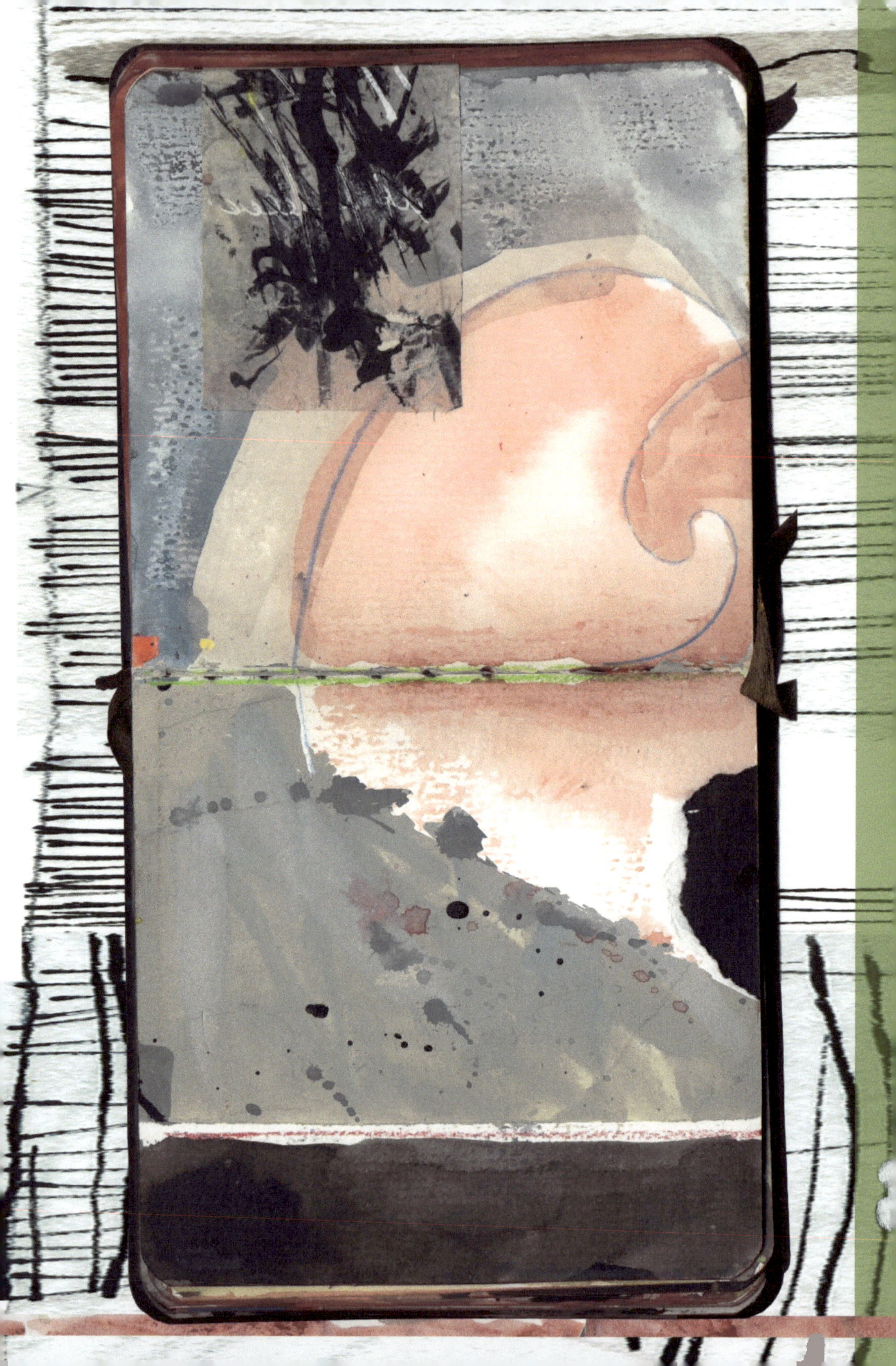

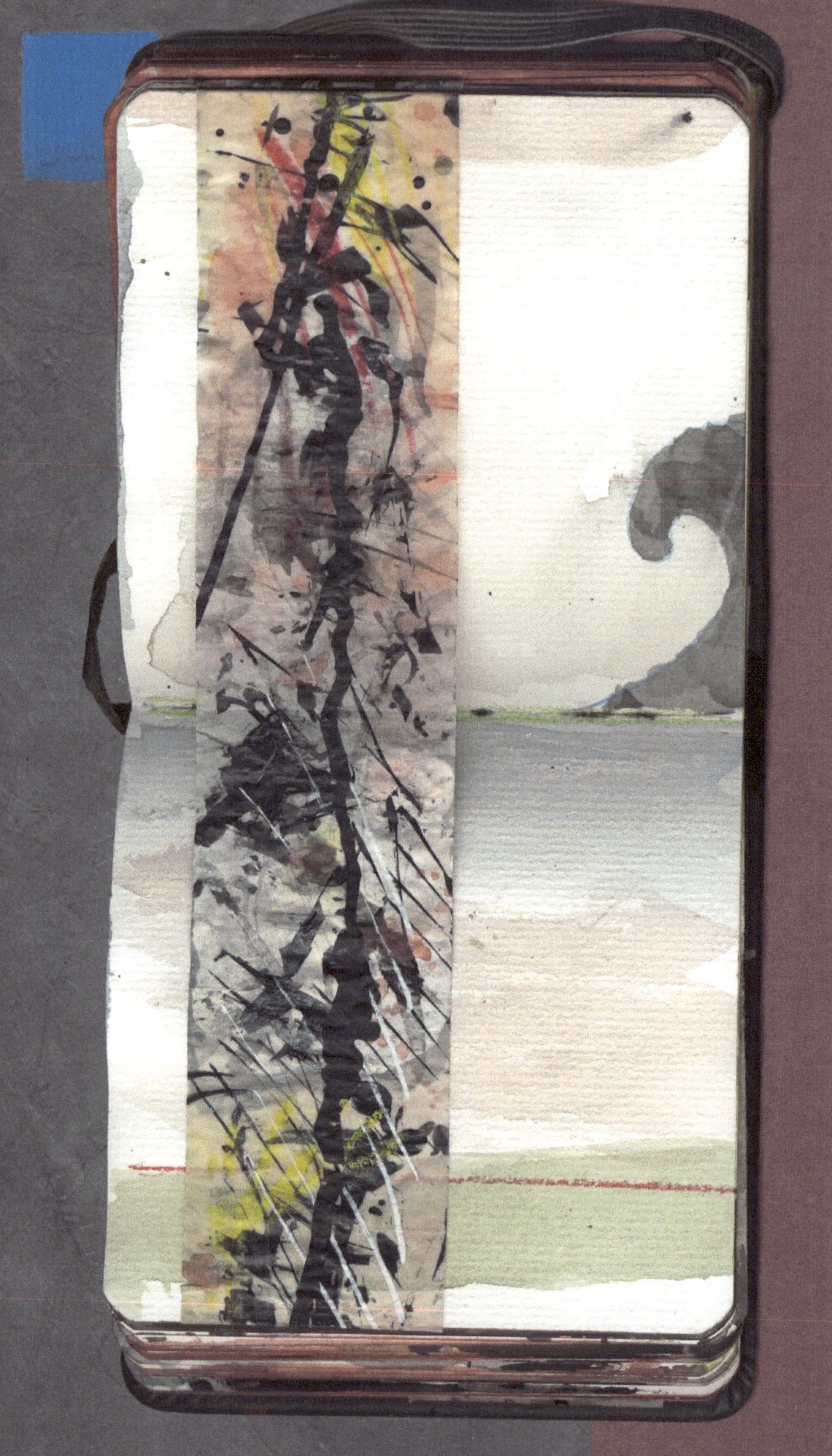

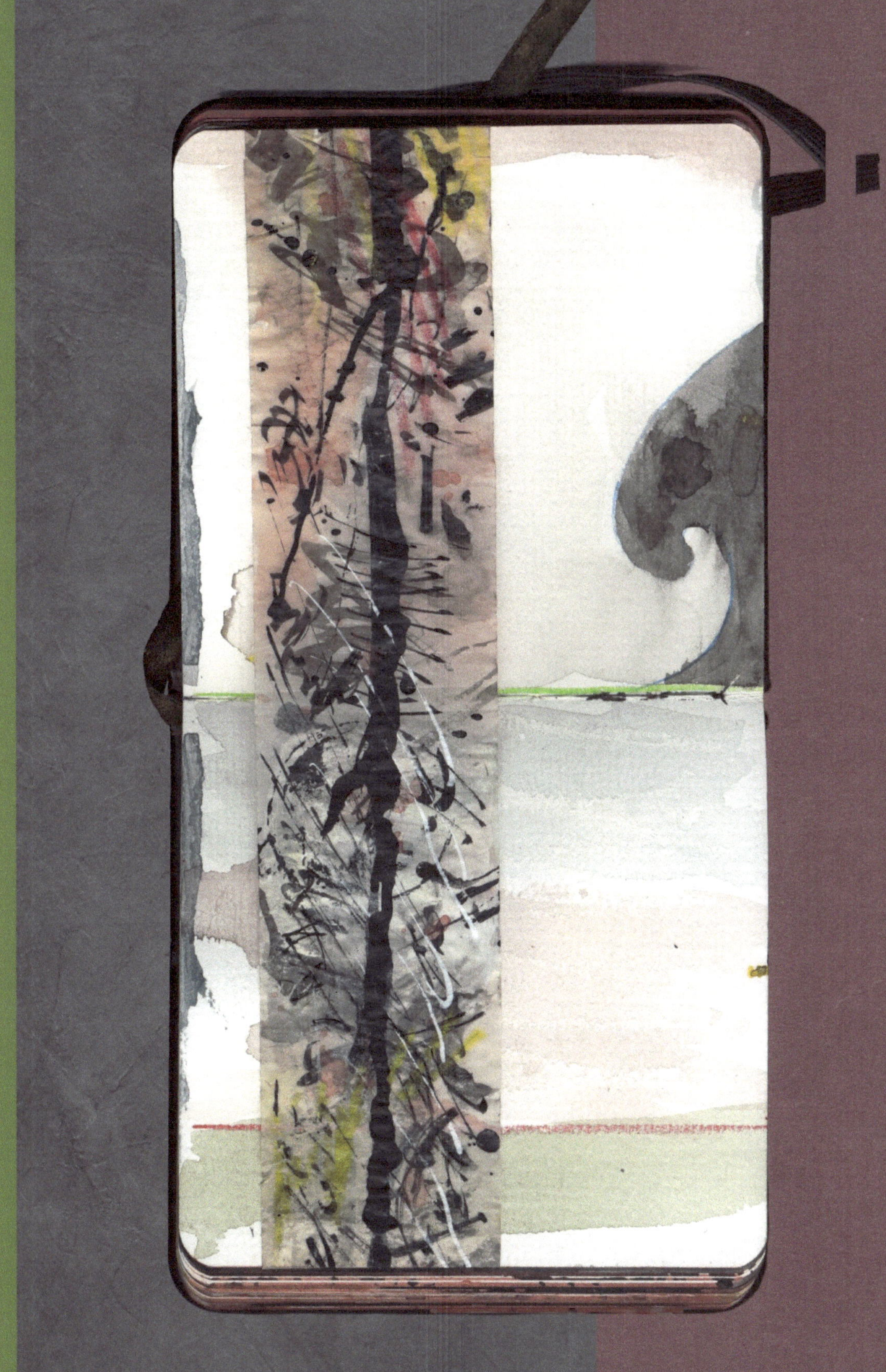

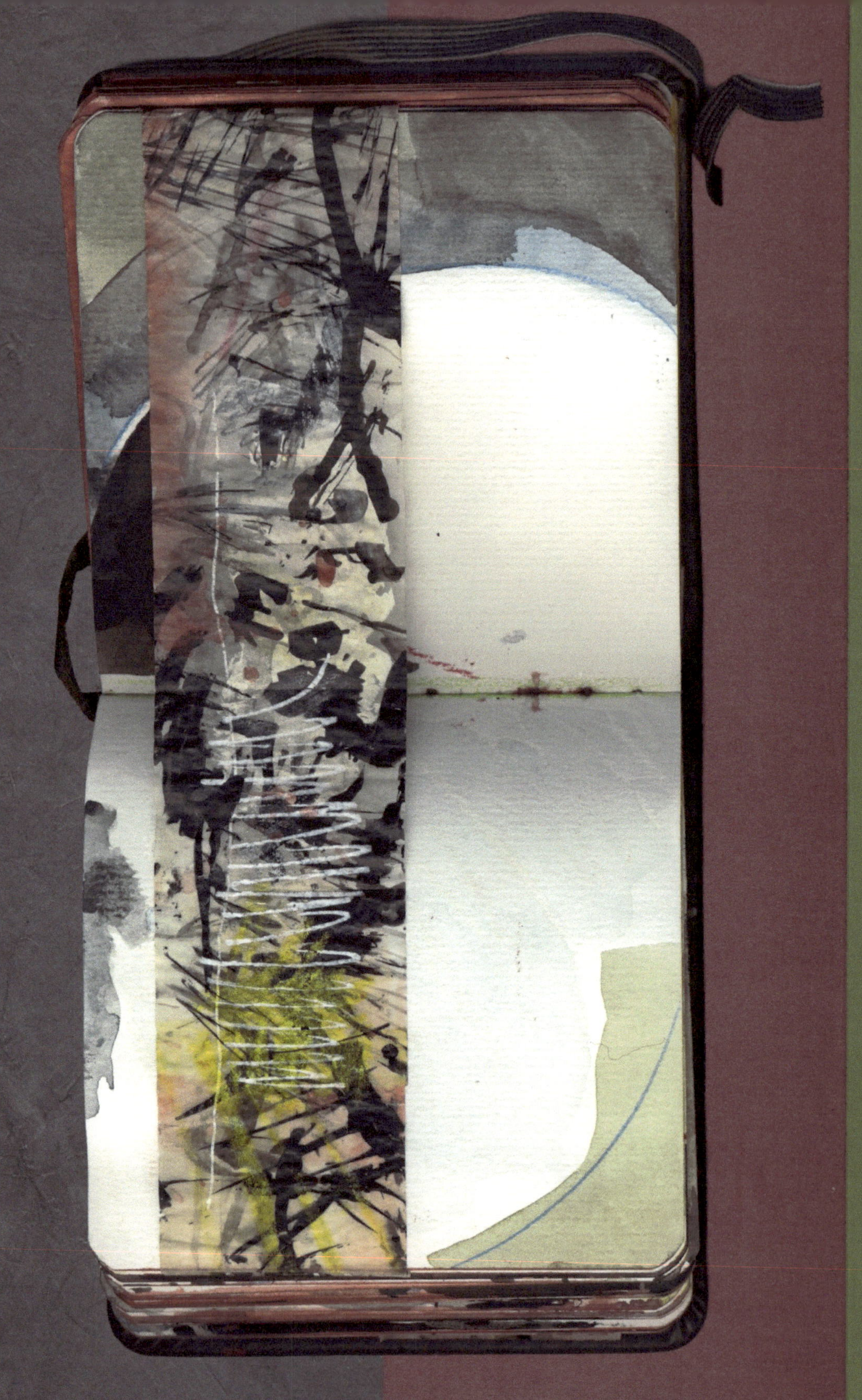

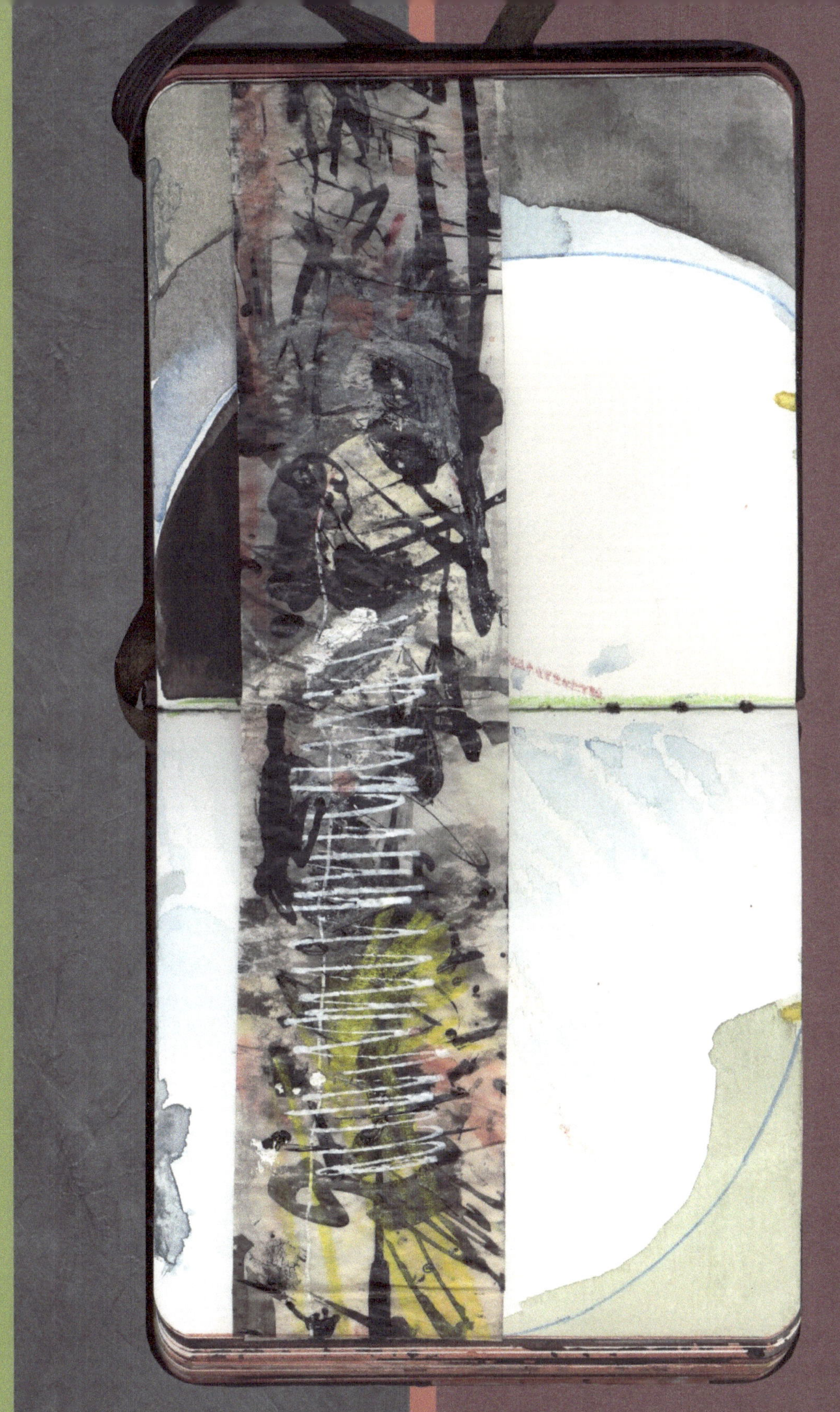

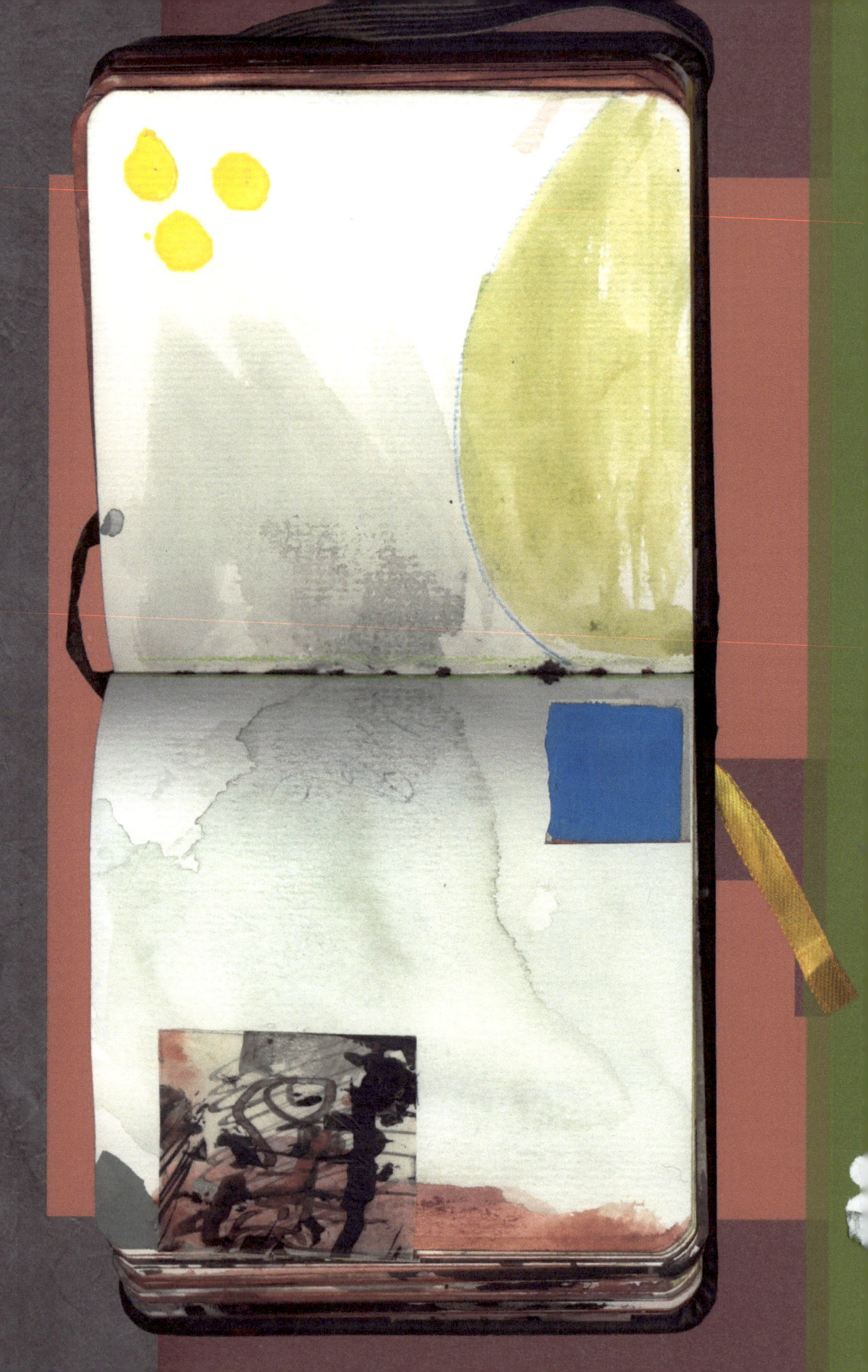

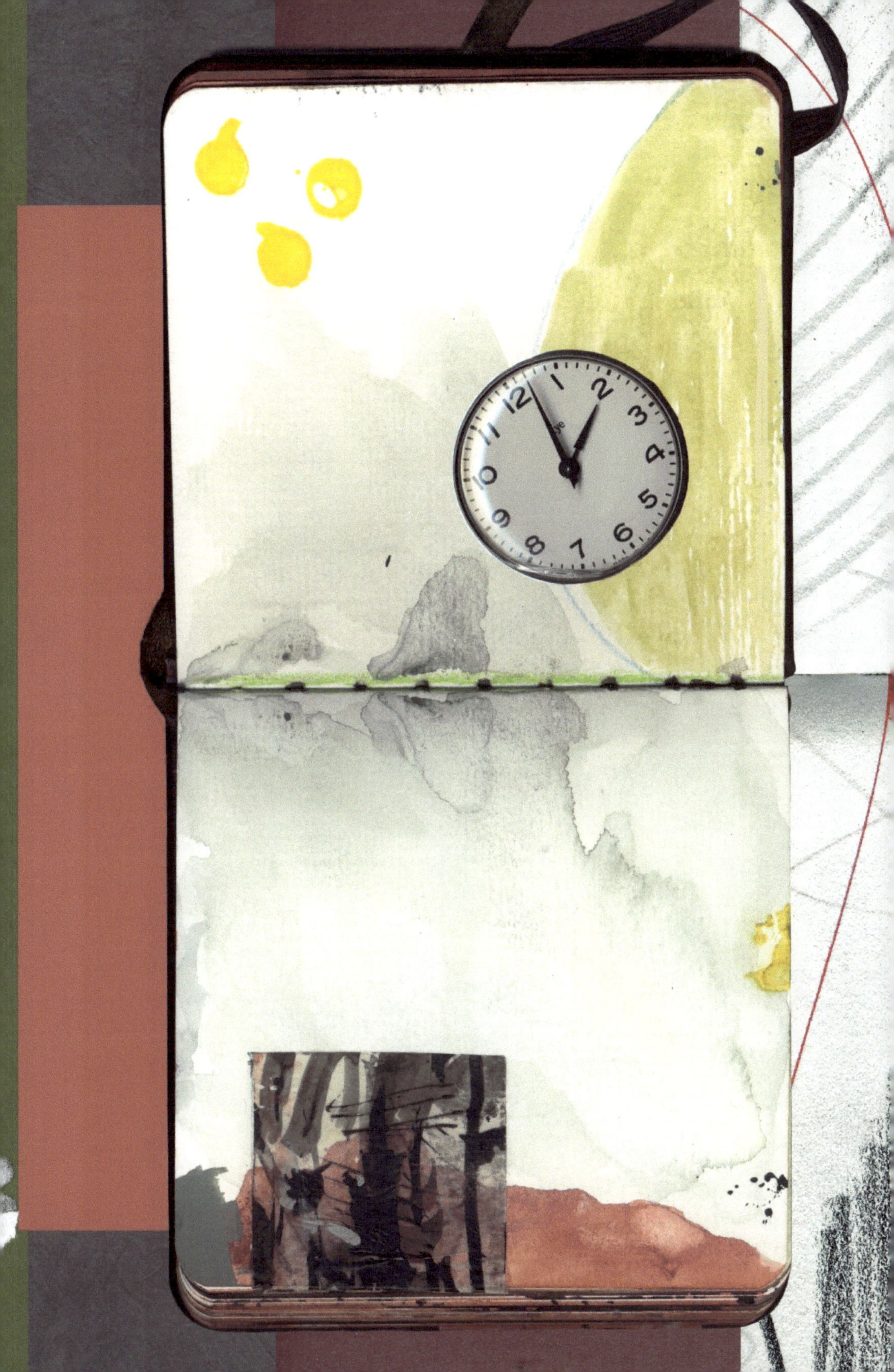

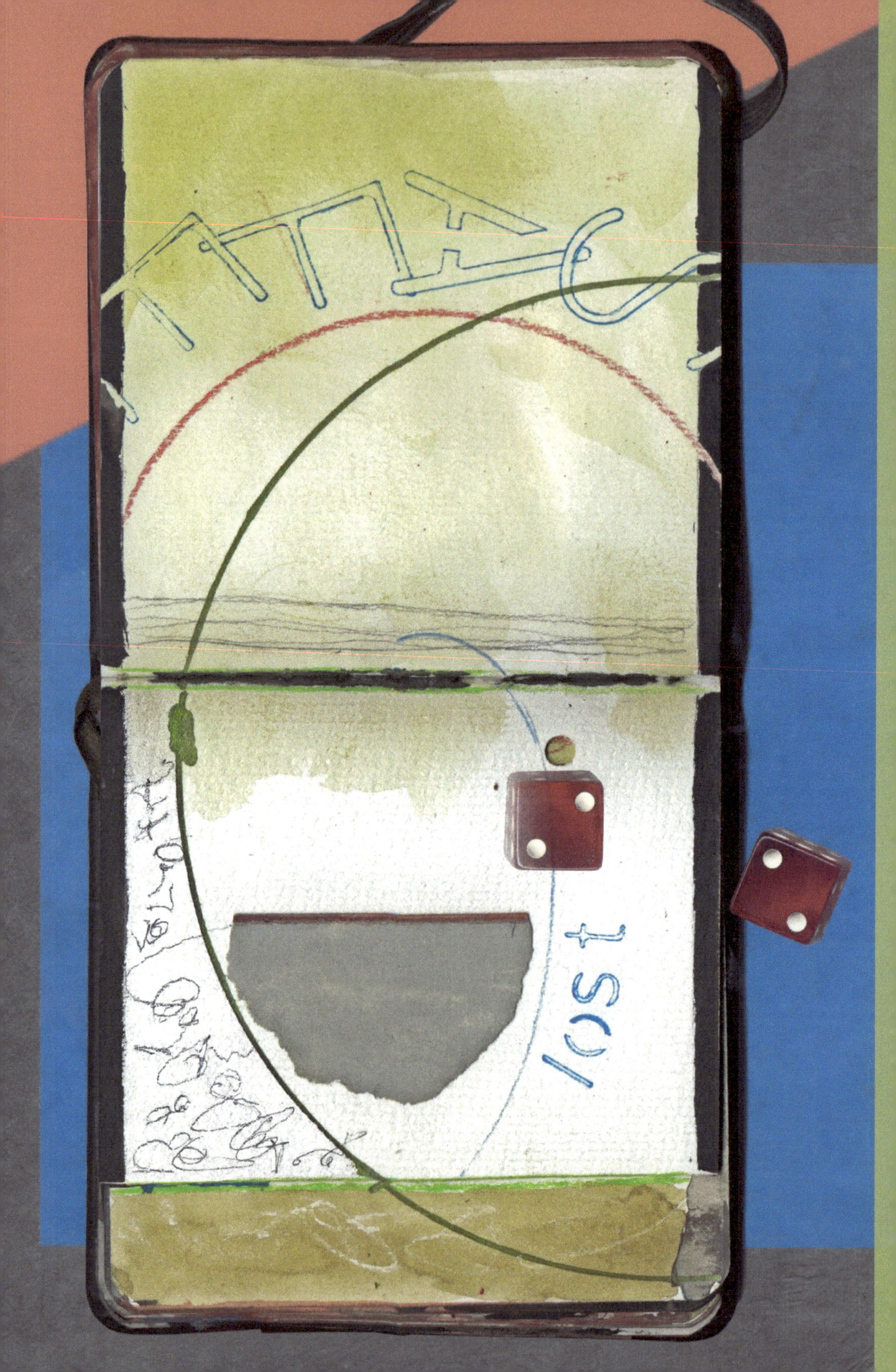

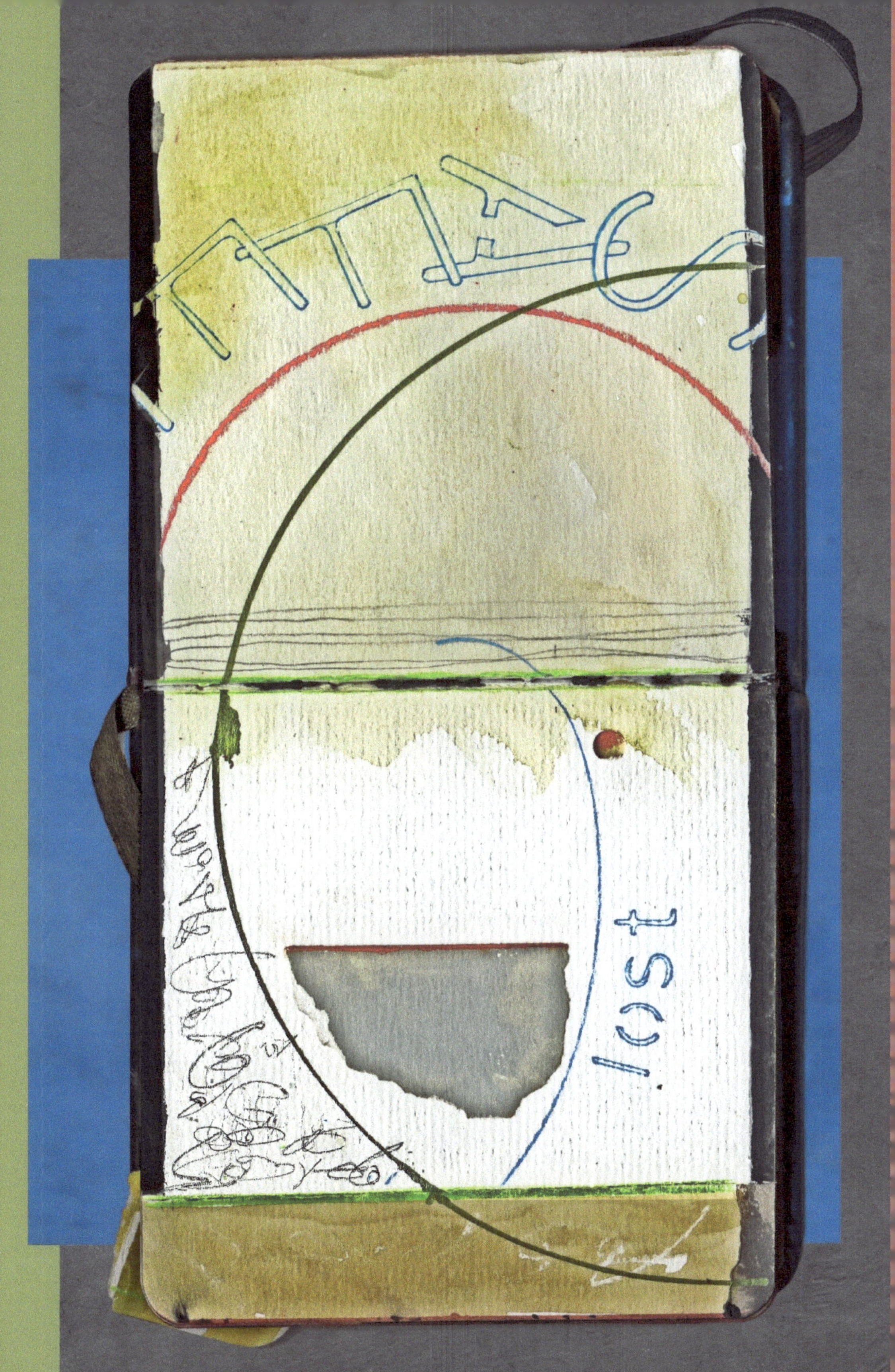
lost

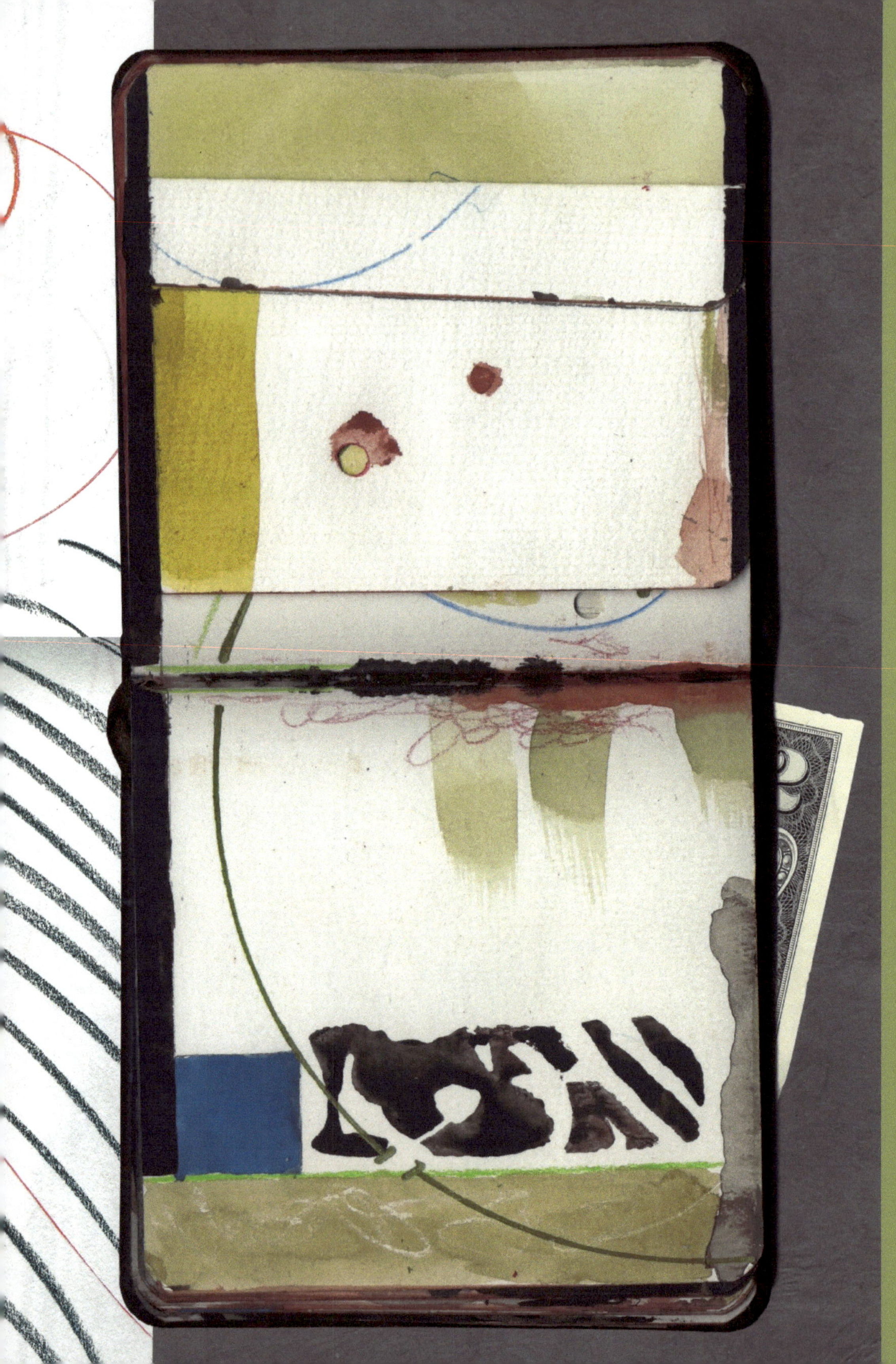

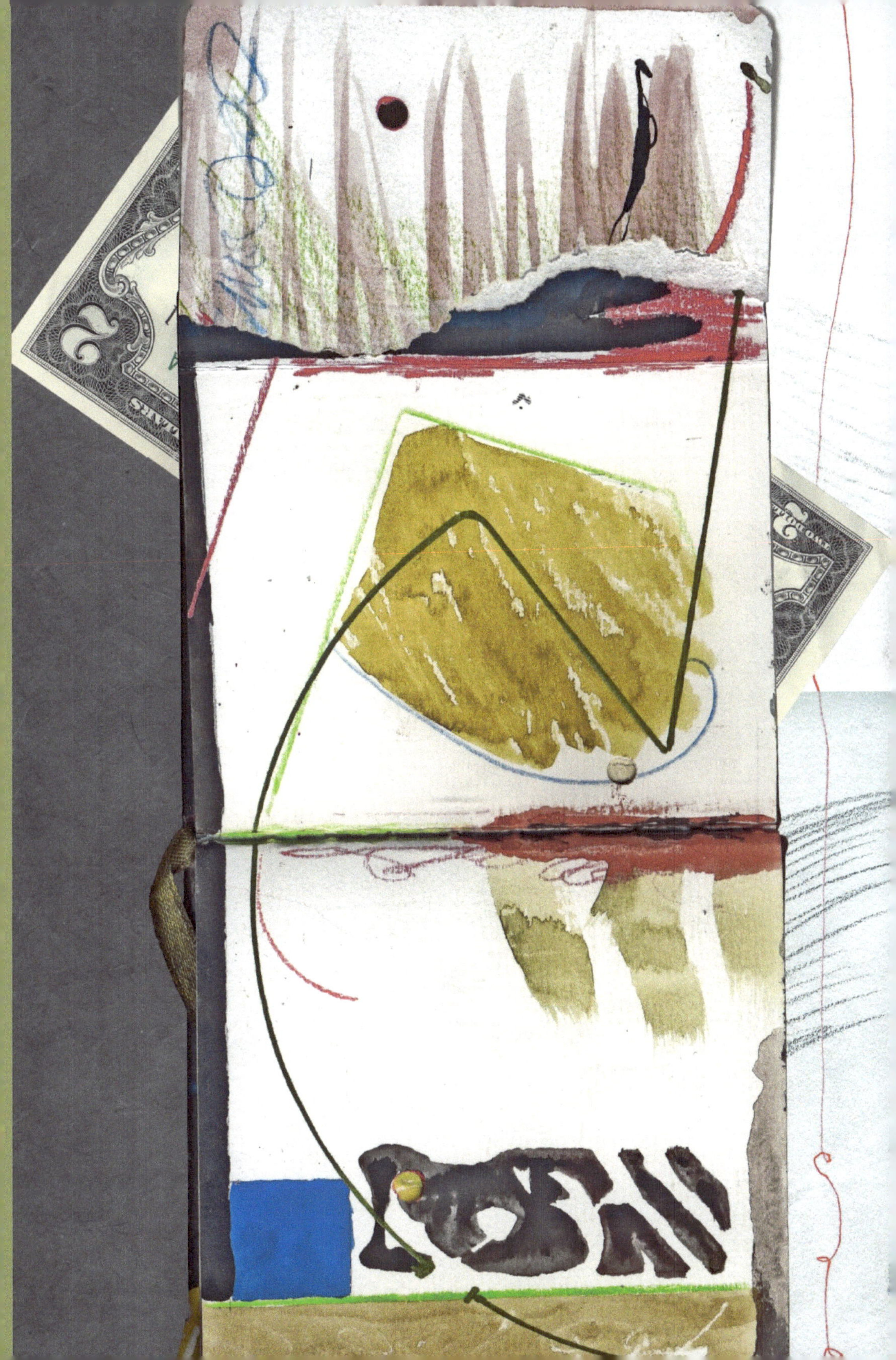

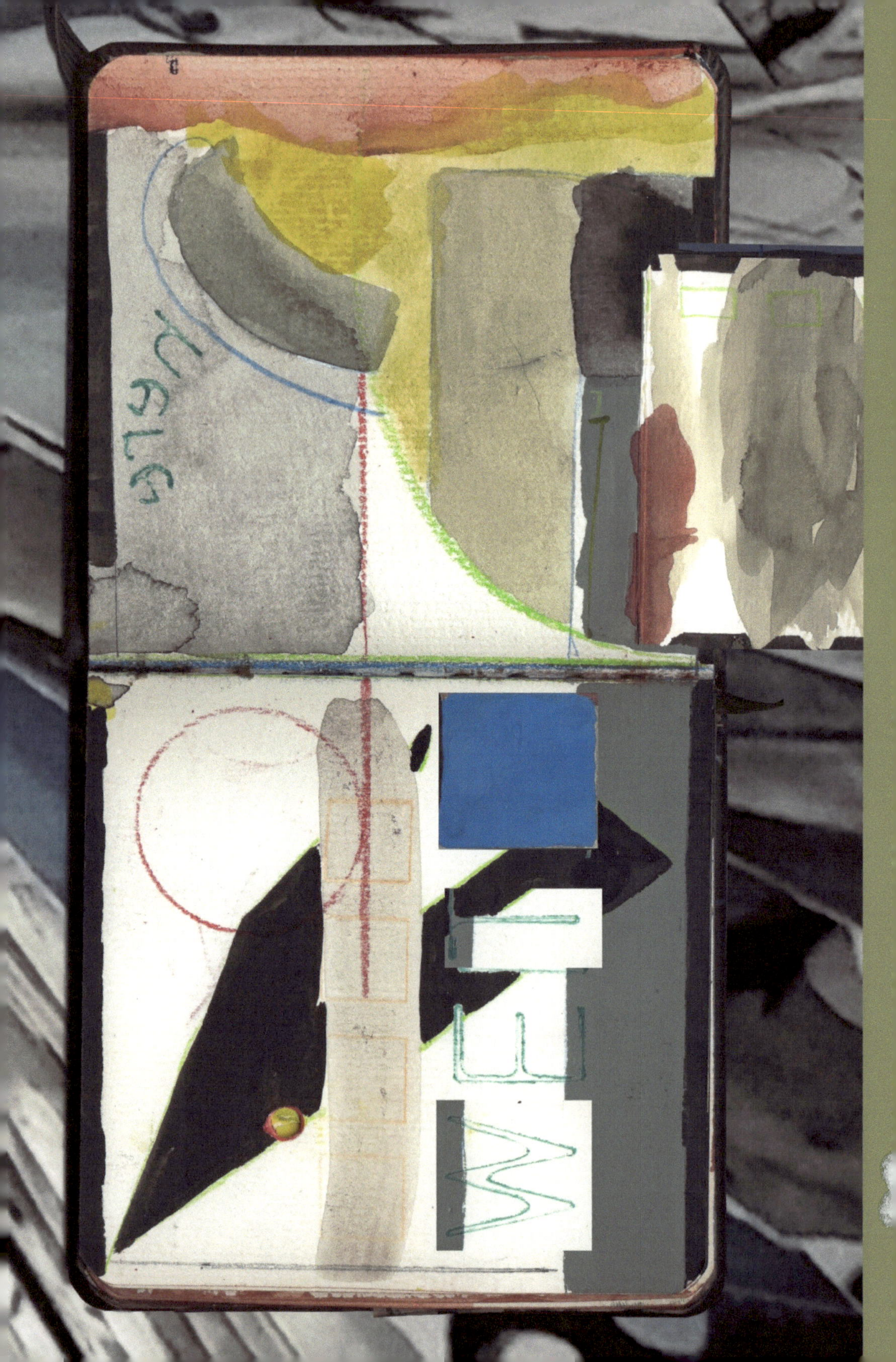

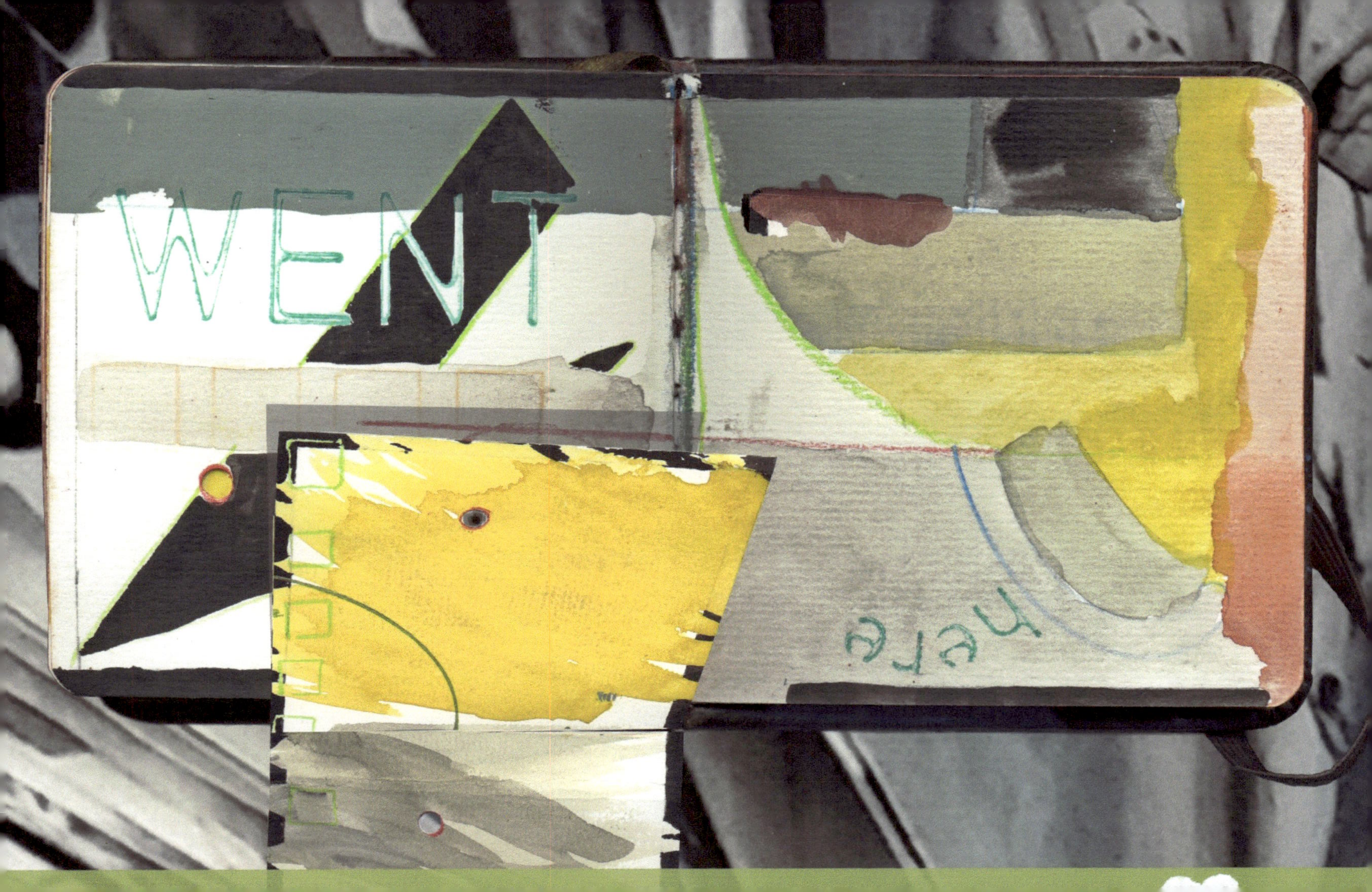
WENT
here

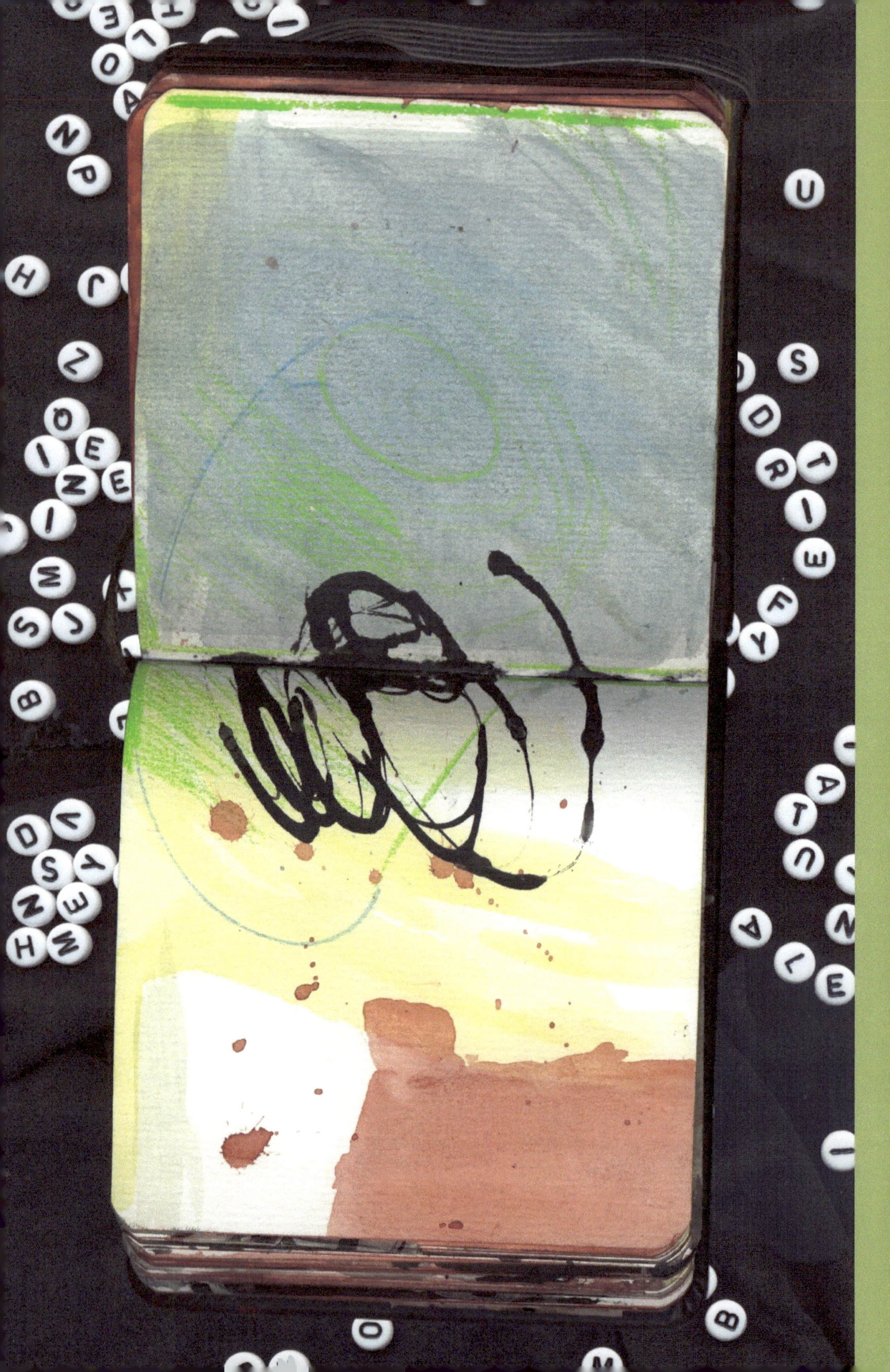

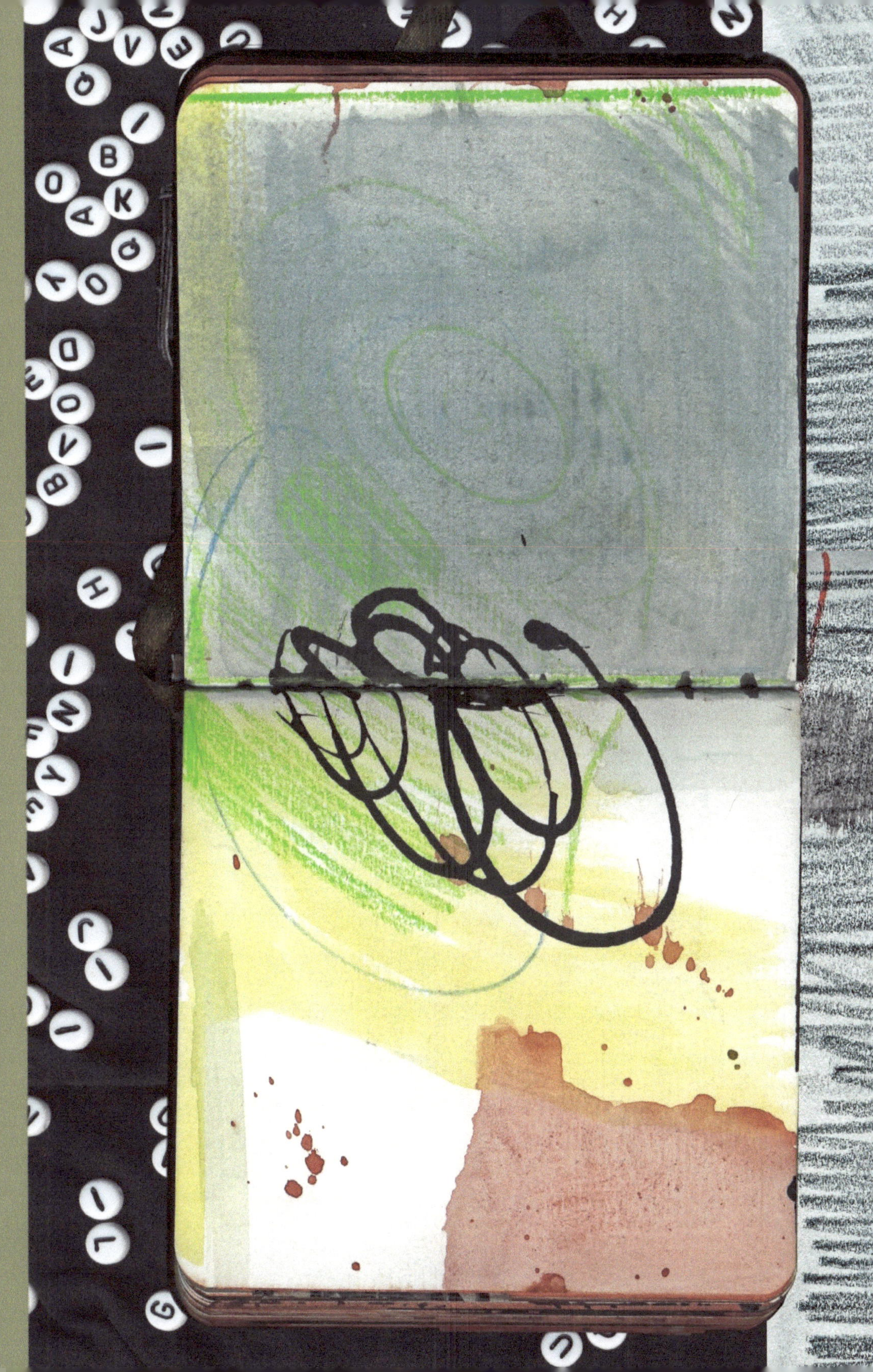

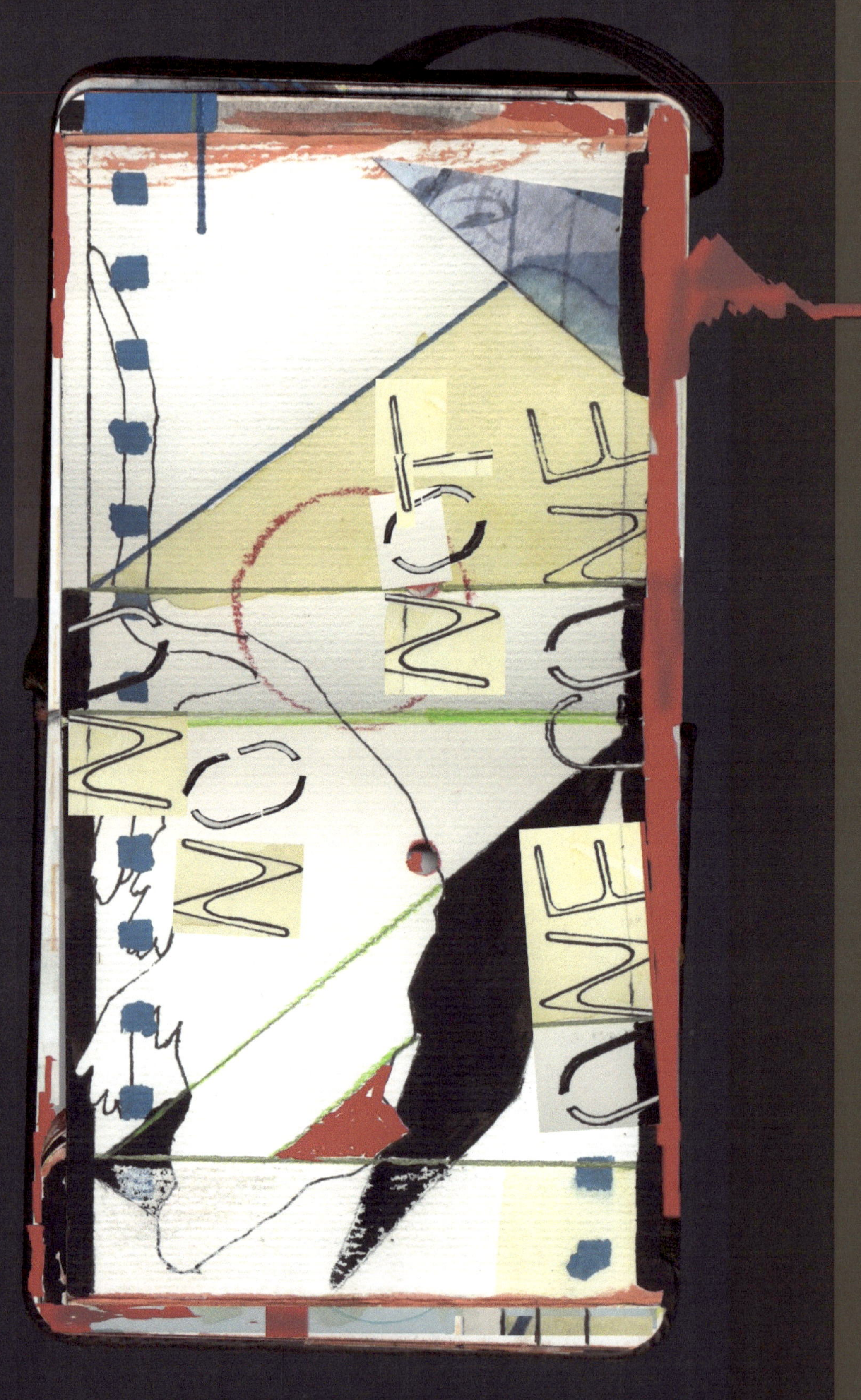

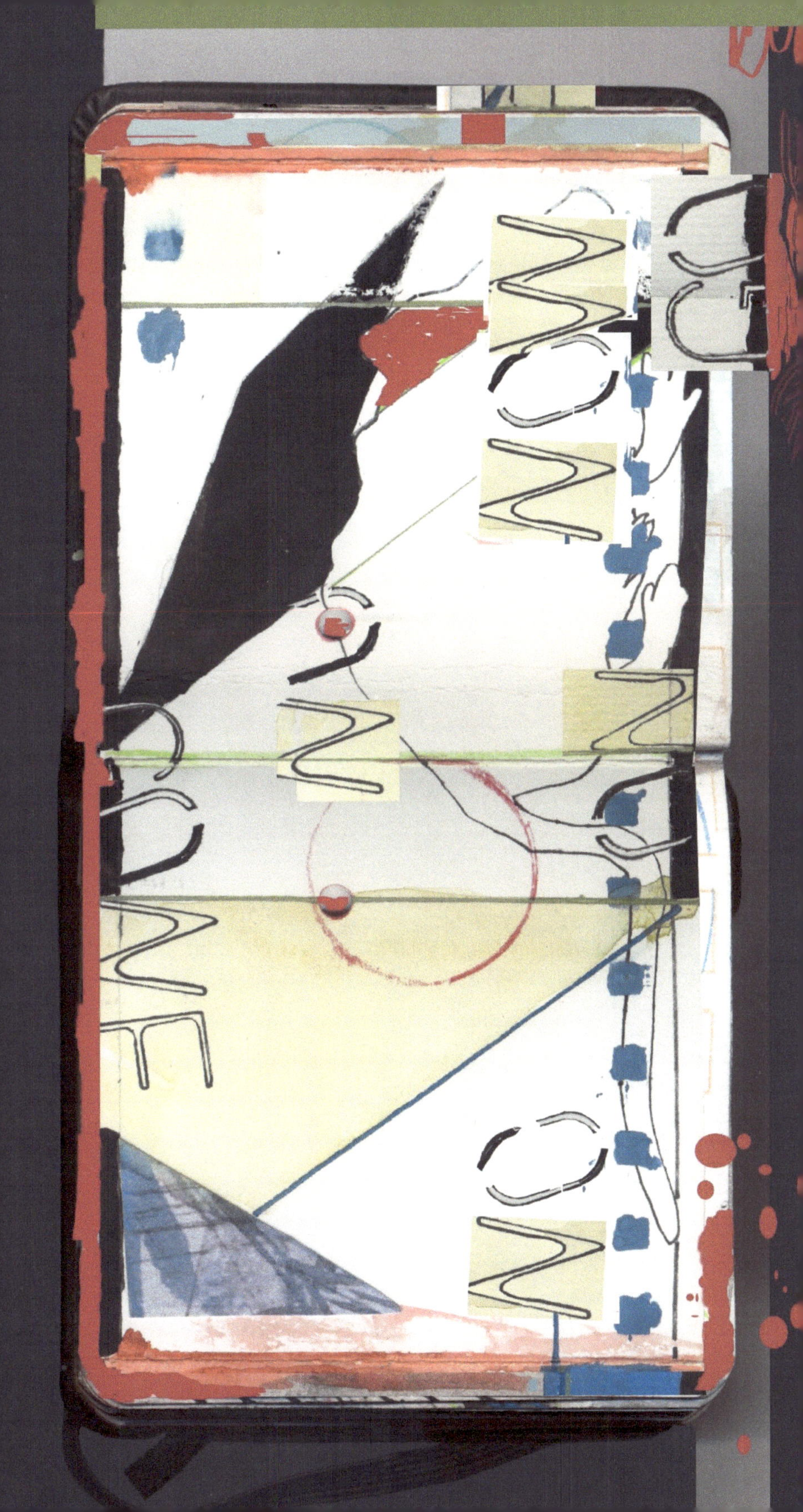

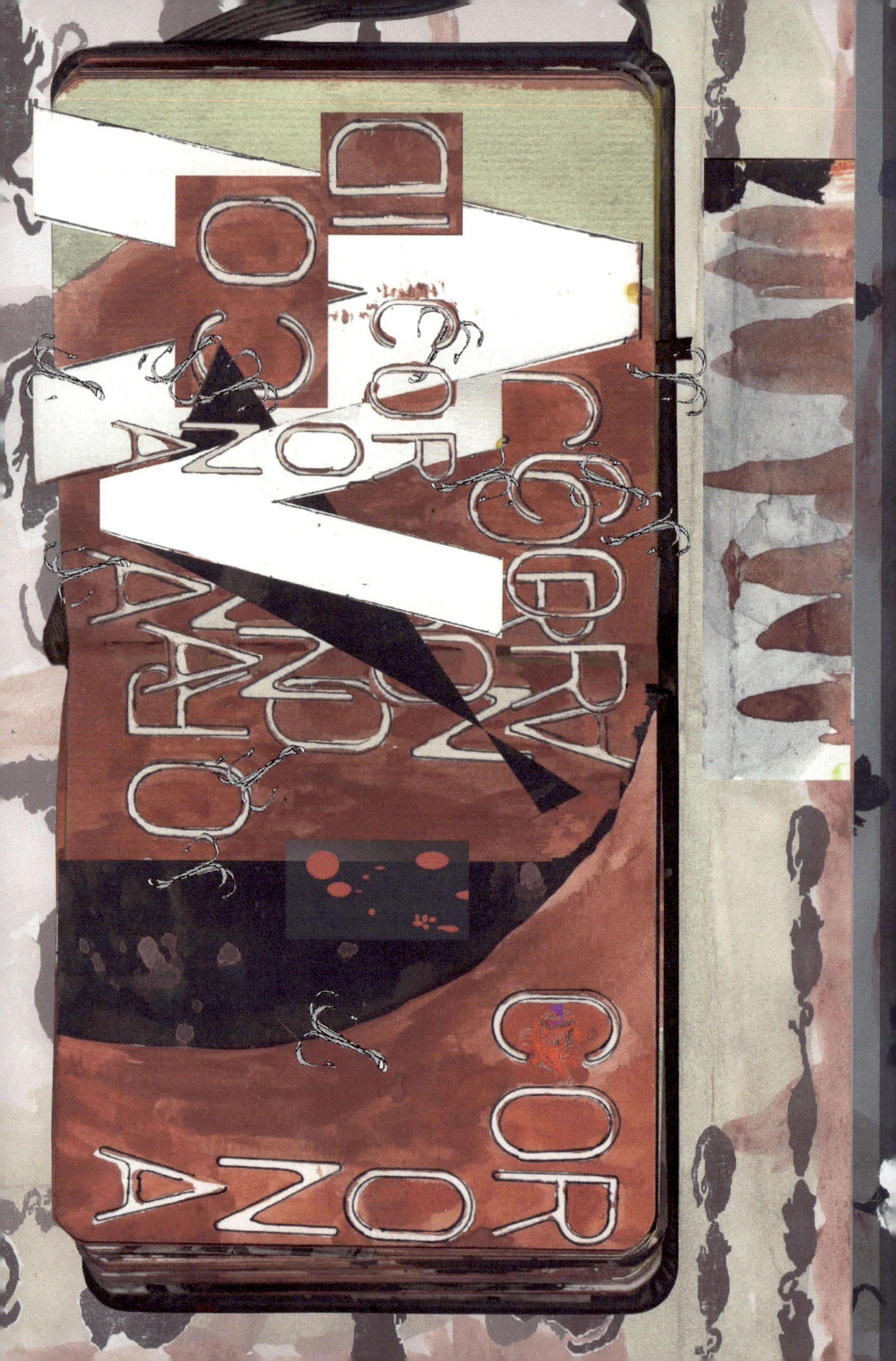

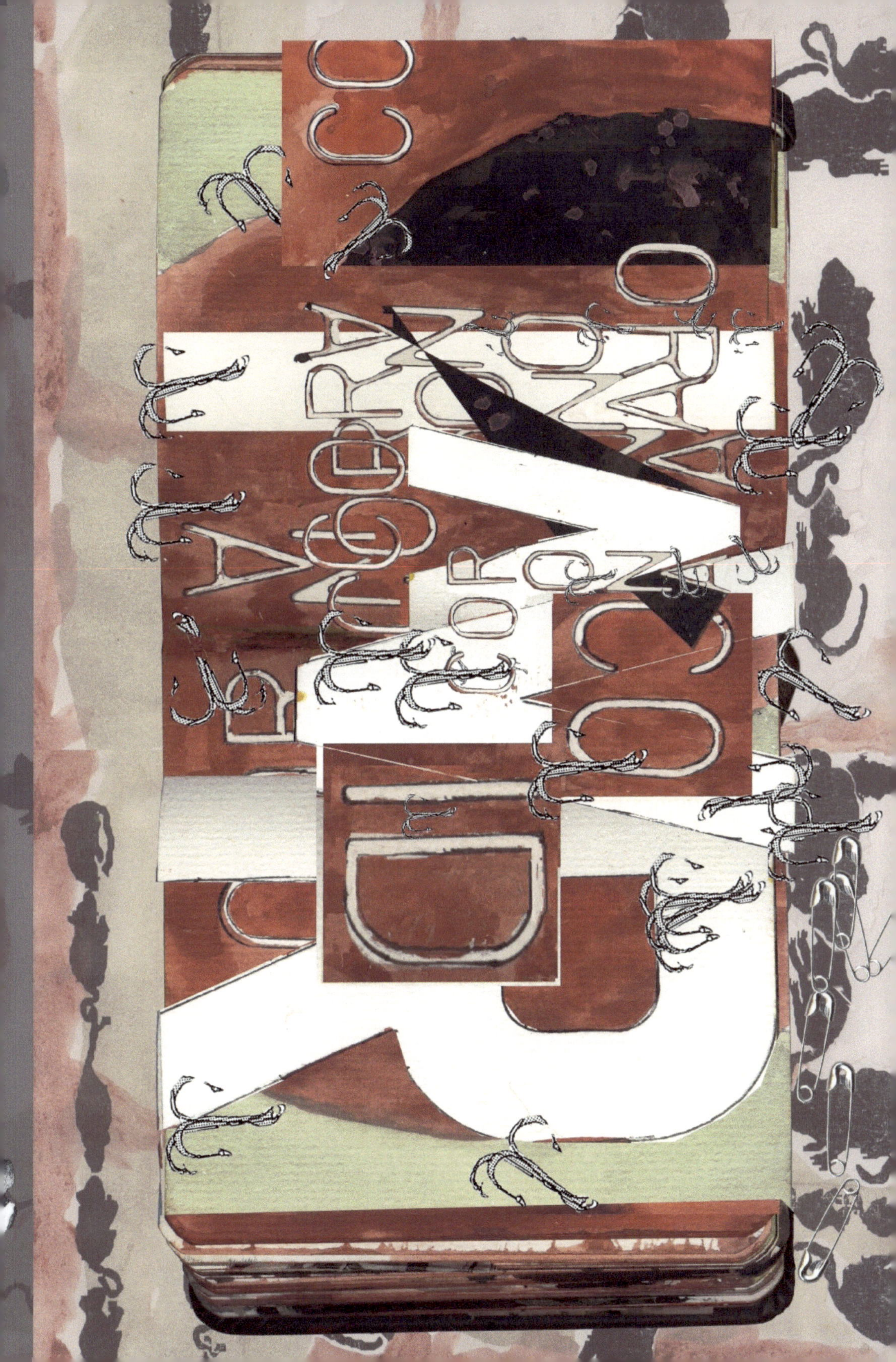

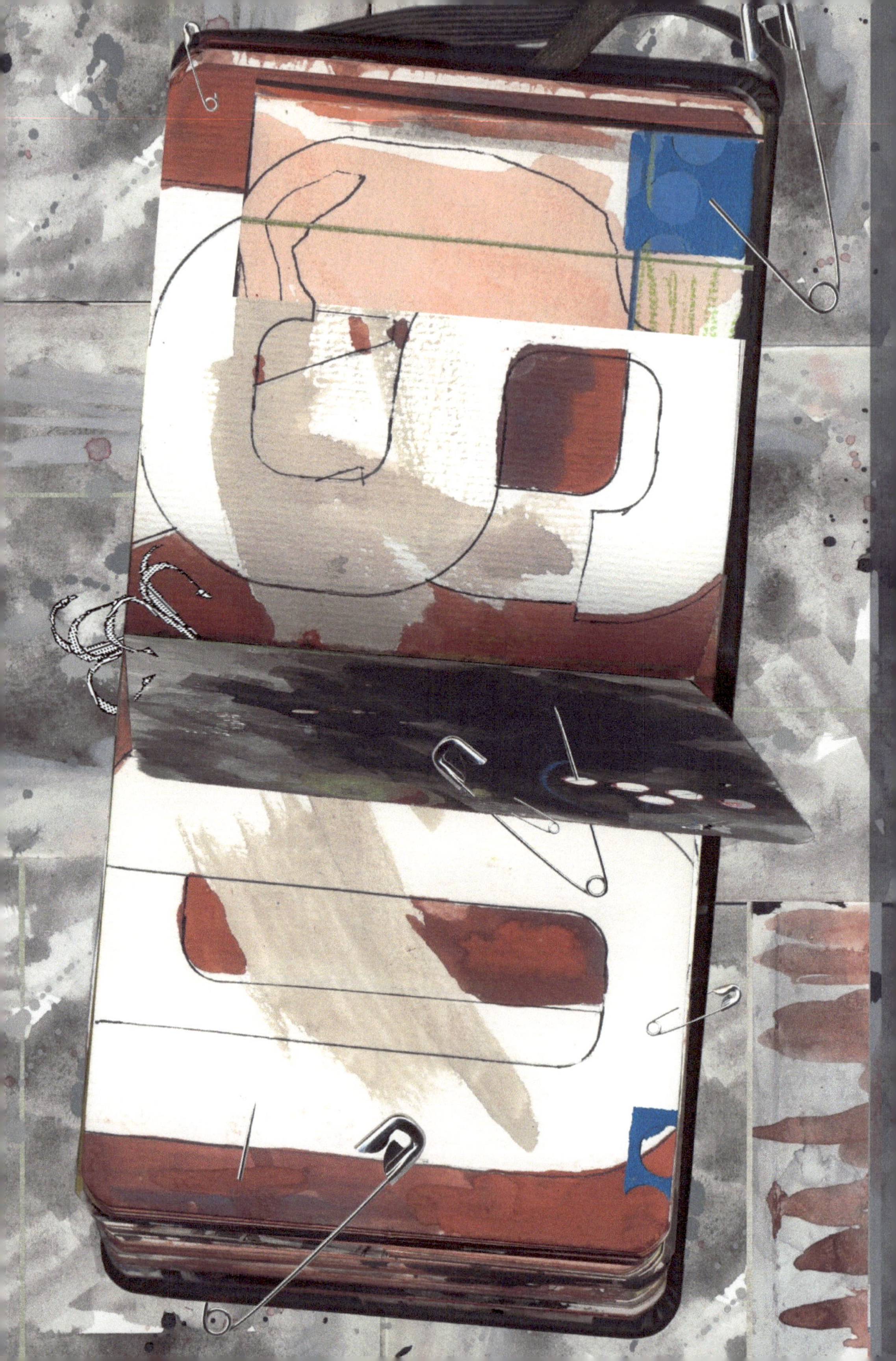

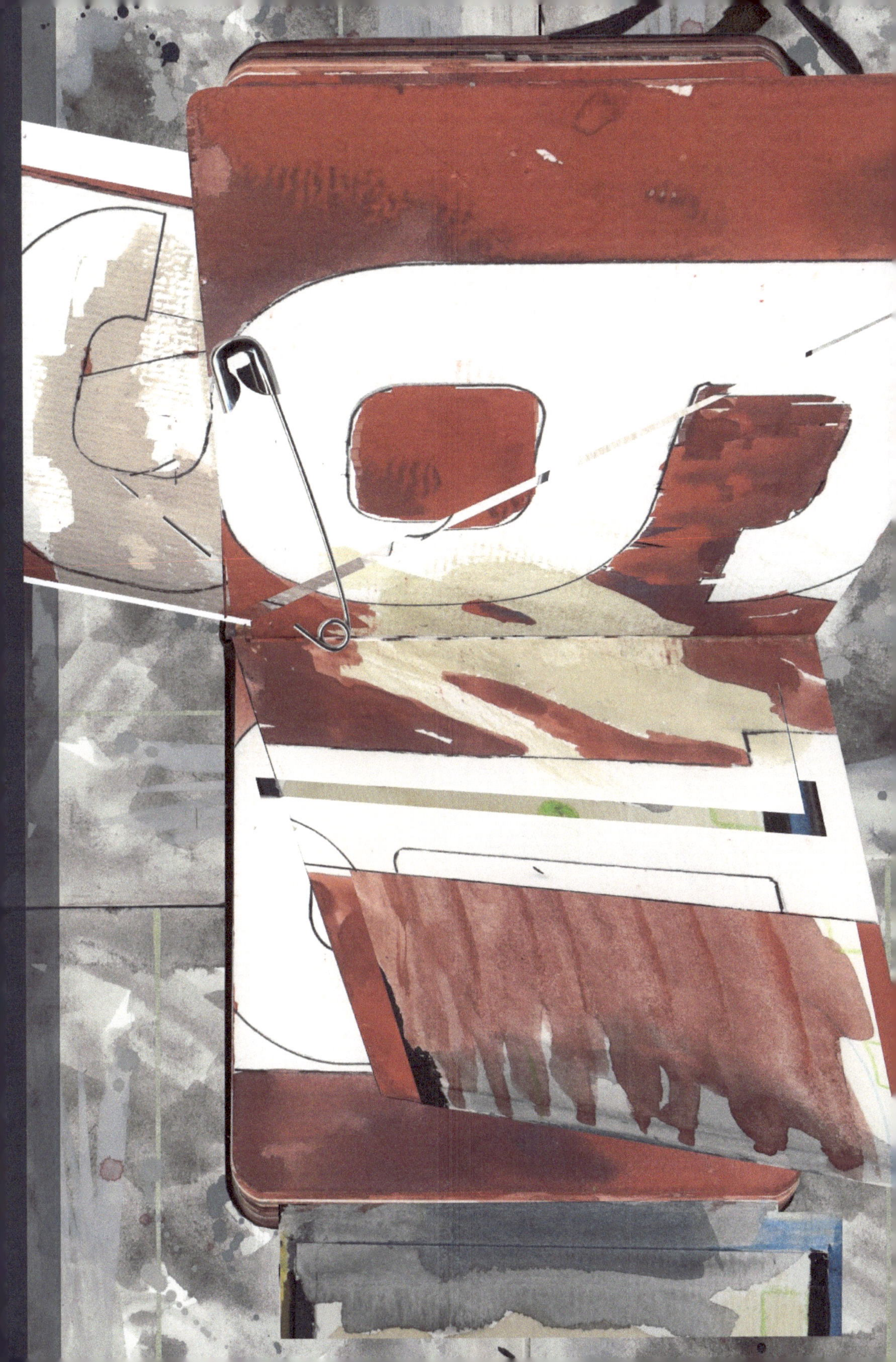

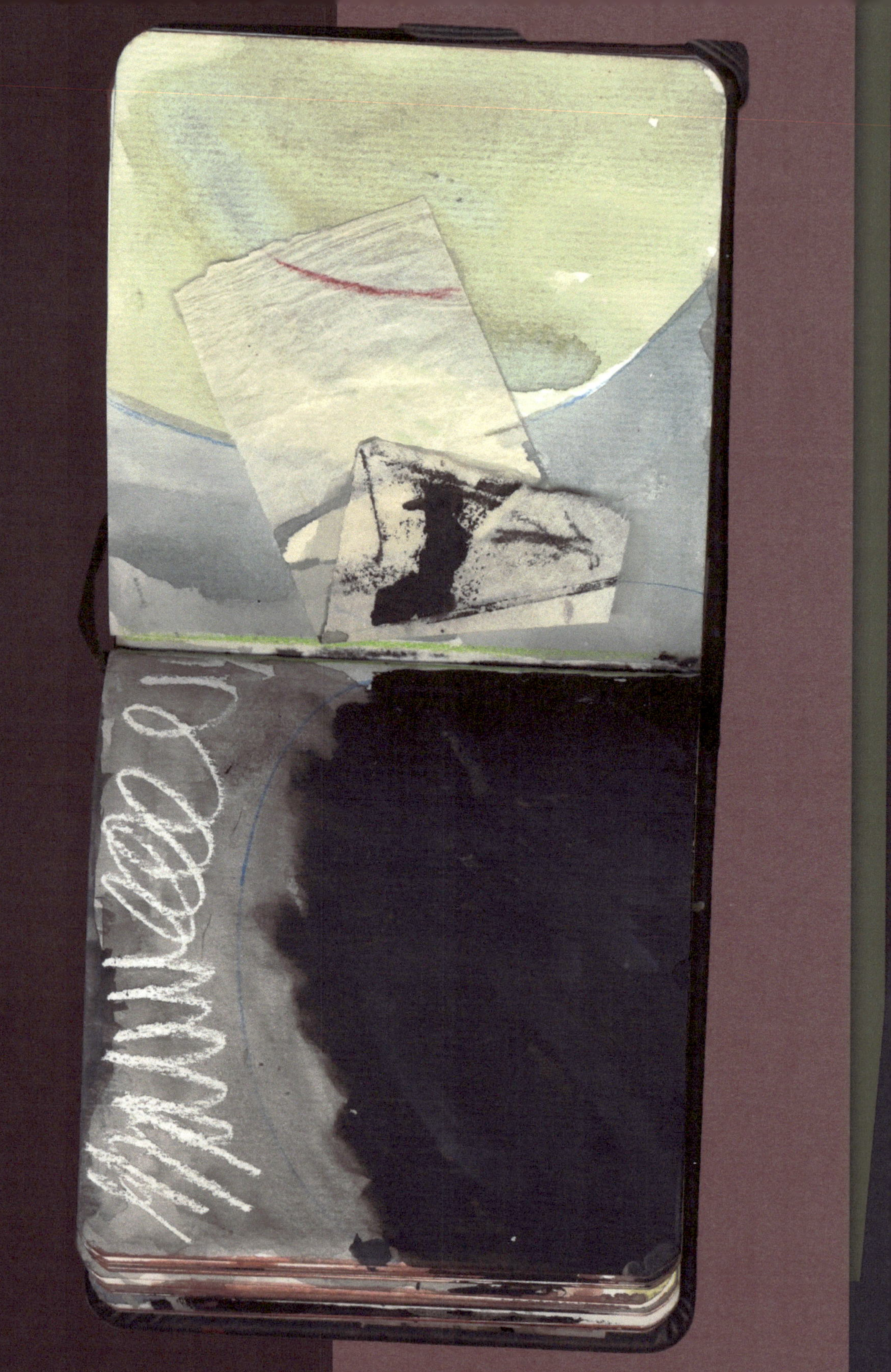

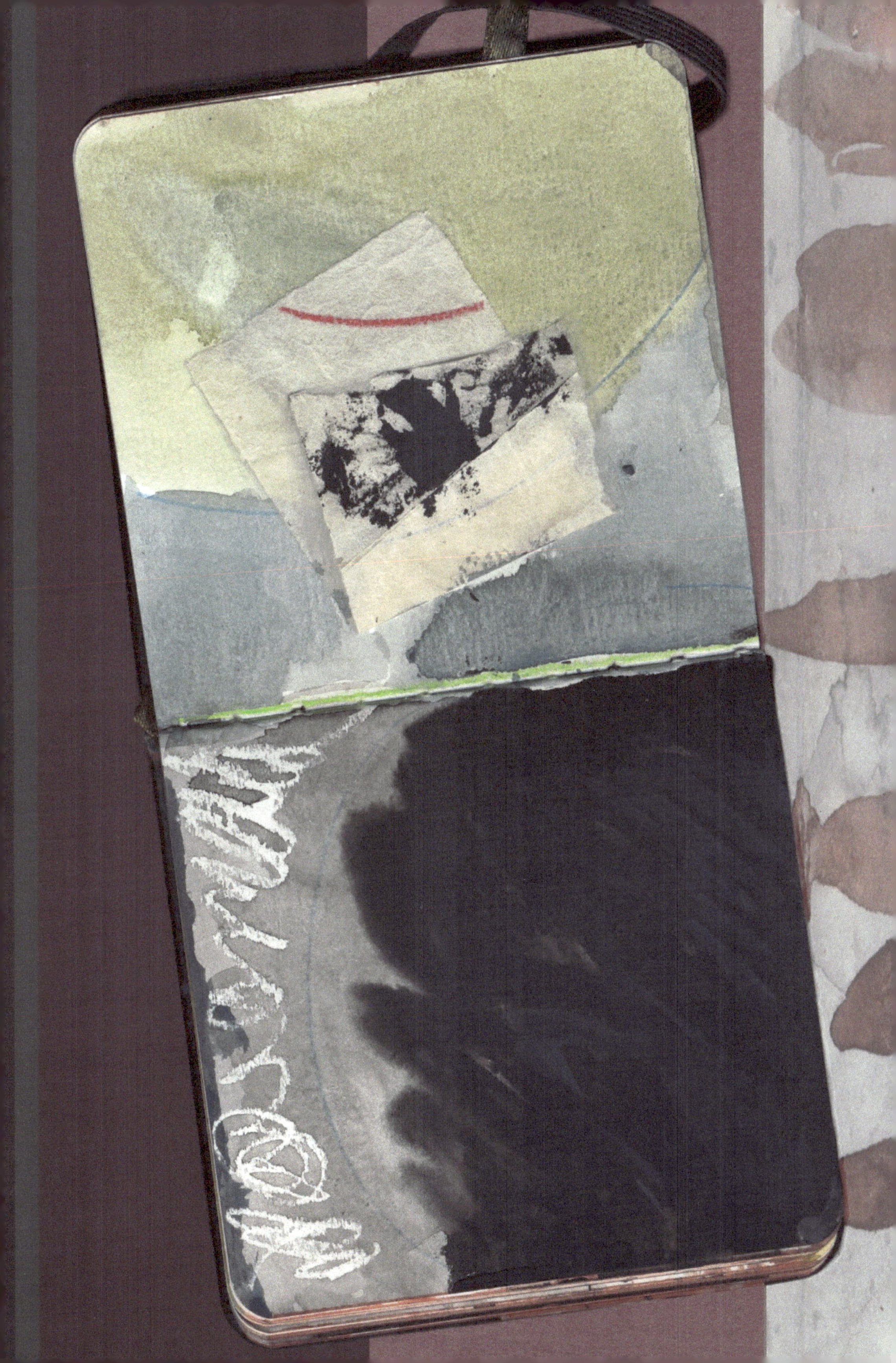

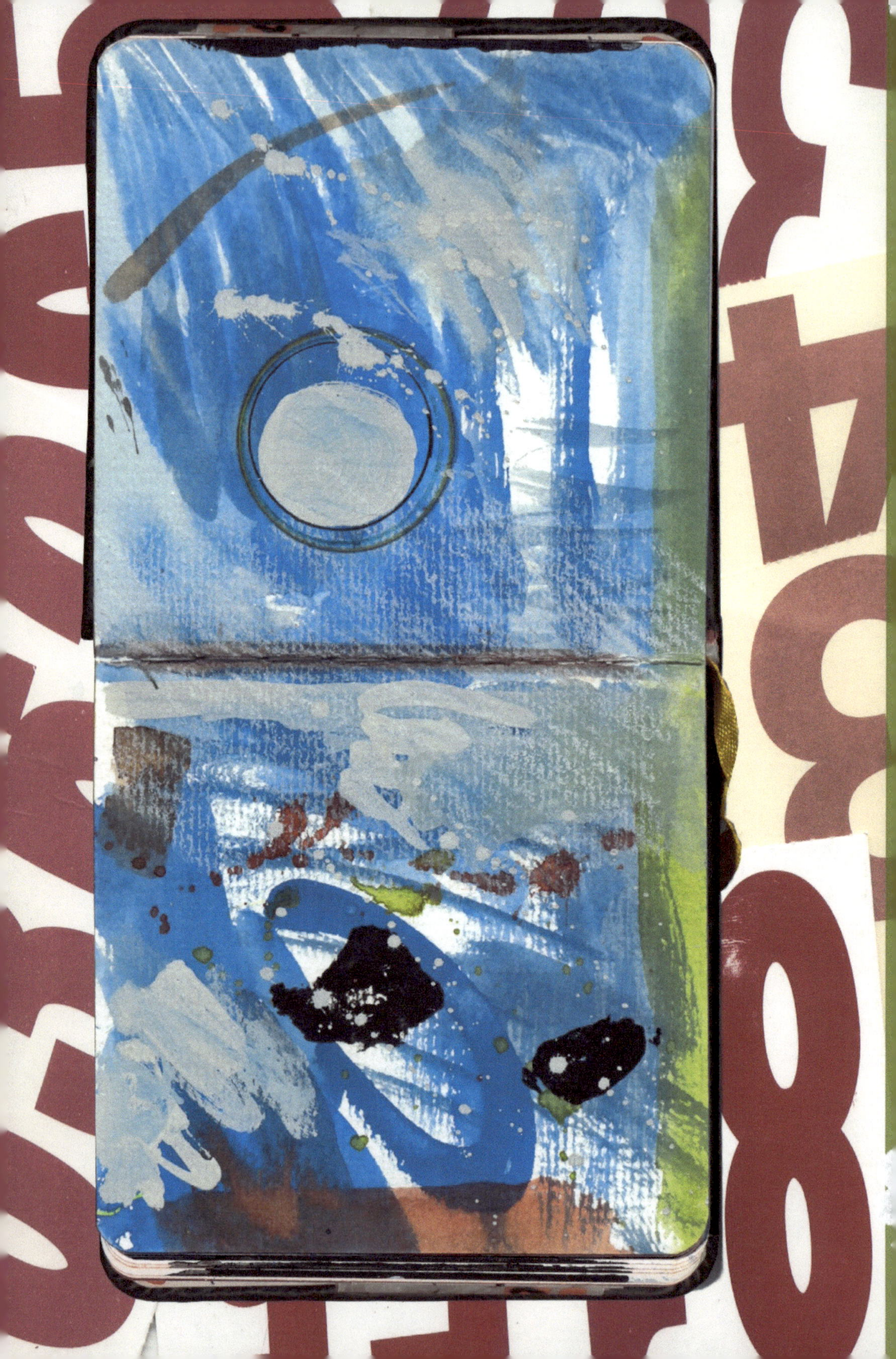

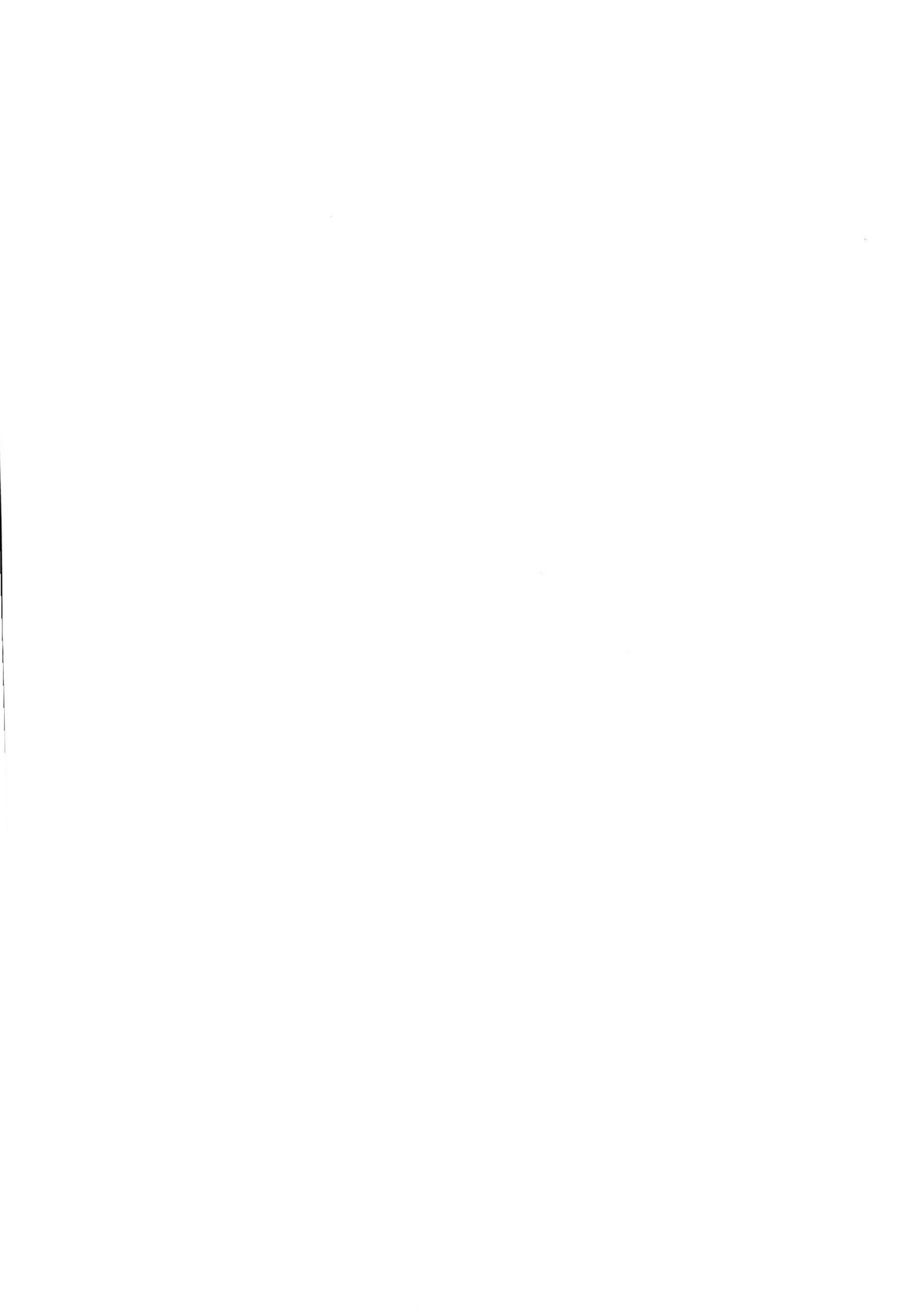

www.ingramcontent.com/pod-product-compliance
Lightning Source LLC
LaVergne TN
LVHW052309100826
845147LV00006B/712

* 9 7 8 1 9 3 8 5 2 1 7 8 2 *